James Monroe

James Madison

Albert Gallatin

THE FIRST REPUBLICANS

Stuart Gerry Brown

As FOUNDERS OF American democracy Jefferson and Madison have never ceased to grow in stature and significance. Most Americans, regardless of party, like to call themselves "Jeffersonians," and our historians, especially in recent years, have given us new and valuable insight into Jefferson and his times. But Jefferson and Madison were members of a great political party— the first Republican Party.

Their ideas were shared by very large numbers of their contemporaries and were modified and qualified by their political colleagues. This book is a systematic study of the ideas and practical programs of the original Republicans. While Jefferson and Madison play leading roles, they are here seen in the perspective of their political and intellectual relations with other great Republicans like James Monroe, Albert Gallatin, and George Mason, and as partisan leaders in the greatest of American political controversies. The period is the thirty years after 1775. The issues are the nature and rights of man, the meaning of the Constitution, the kind of domestic policy and of foreign policy proper to a free republic, the relation of religion to the state, and the place of education in a free, republican society. All these are studied from the point of view of the old Republican Party. Their ideas are analysed and their achievement assessed against two on the philosophy of Josiah Royce which are described on the back of this jacket. Dr. Brown is professor of Citizenship and American Culture in the Maxwell School of Citizenship at Syracuse.

The First Republicans

THE FIRST
REPUBLICANS

Political Philosophy and Public Policy
in the Party of Jefferson and Madison

STUART GERRY BROWN

Professor of Citizenship and American Culture
Maxwell School of Citizenship
Syracuse University

SYRACUSE UNIVERSITY PRESS 1954

Preface

THIS BOOK IS a study in the history of partisan ideas. It inevitably takes account of many important events in the founding years of the American Republic, but it makes no pretense to a place among full-dress political histories. It deals, often at length, with individual men like Jefferson, Madison, Monroe, or Gallatin, but there is no attempt at a rounded estimate of any. The purpose of the book, rather, is to extricate from the complex history of the thirty-odd years after 1775 those essential ideas which bound together the republican faction, and to study the relations of these ideas to the concrete policies and programs which united the republicans in political action and characterized them as the Republican Party.

While the point of view throughout is that of the Republicans themselves, and their bias is a predominant theme, I have tried to assess the ideas and policies of their Federalist opponents fairly. Thus, though I have tried to suggest the extent and quality of the lasting contributions made by the Republicans, I hope that I have made no exaggerated claims. On the other hand, I have not disguised my sympathies with Republicanism, and if the reader is moved to construct his own estimate of the Federalists as a counterweight I shall be well content. The purpose of the book will be realized if the reader finds in these pages a logical articulation of certain great ideas which the old Republicans took where they found them and built into a system of free government and a free way of life.

v

The Bibliographical Note at the end of the book, as well as the text itself, will tell the specialist that while I have rested the whole book on the original documents, I have made liberal use of the original researches and the new evaluations of several distinguished scholars. I have felt that the specialized studies of men like Irving Brant, Dumas Malone, and Leonard White are a standing challenge to the generalist student of the history of ideas to make full use of them in a fresh look at larger perspectives. In particular, I should say that my own studies of the original documents have led me to accept, with full conviction, a number of Mr. Brant's controversial findings, such as Madison's roles in drafting the Virginia Declaration of Rights and the First Amendment to the Constitution.

To follow a friend's work in all its stages of growth word for word, with a critical and appraising eye, is no light burden, and acknowledgement in a preface is meager thanks. But T. V. Smith will, I think, accept these sentences with the same generosity which persuaded him to share with me his wisdom and his insight. I wish also to express my gratitude, for many long and valuable conversations, to my friends Professors Edward E. Palmer and Webb S. Fiser, and Dean Paul H. Appleby.

Finally, if this re-examination of early American Republicanism suggests to any reader a purpose in re-examining that present-day "Republicanism" which came into power while I was at work on this book, or that panoply of "Jeffersonian Democracy" in which many very conservative politicians enshroud themselves, I can have no objection.

S. G. B.

Maxwell School of Citizenship,
Syracuse University,
January 29, 1954

Contents

And so whoever has the legislative or supreme power of any commonwealth is bound to govern by established standing laws, promulgated and known to the people, and not by extemporary decrees; by indifferent and upright judges, who are to decide controversies by those laws; and to employ the force of the community at home only in the execution of such laws, or abroad, to prevent or redress foreign injuries, and secure the community from inroads and invasion. And all this to be directed to no other end but the peace, safety, and public good of the people.

— John Locke, 1689.

REPUBLICAN—*Mysteries belong to religion, not to government;· to the ways of the Almighty, not to the works of man. And in religion itself there is nothing mysterious to its author; the mystery lies in the dimness of the human sight. So in the institutions of man let there be no mystery, unless for those inferior beings endowed with a ray perhaps of the twilight vouchsafed to the first order of terrestrial creation.*

ANTI-REPUBLICAN—*You are destitute, I perceive, of every quality of a good citizen, or rather of a good subject. You have neither the light of faith nor the spirit of obedience. I denounce you to the government as an accomplice of atheism and anarchy.*

REPUBLICAN—*And I forbear to denounce you to the people, though a blasphemer of their rights and an idolater of tyranny. Liberty disdains to persecute.*

— James Madison, 1792.

It is a singular anxiety which some people have that we should all think alike. Would the world be more beautiful were all our faces alike? were our tempers, our talents, our tastes, our forms, our wishes, aversions and pursuits cast exactly in the same mold? If no varieties existed in the animal, vegetable or mineral creation, but all move strictly uniform, catholic & orthodox, what a world of physical and moral monotony it would be! These are the absurdities into which those run who usurp the throne of God and dictate to Him what He should have done.

— Thomas Jefferson, 1817.

*... all men are by nature equally free and independent, and have
certain inherent rights, of which, when they enter into a state of
society, they cannot by any compact deprive or divest their posterity; namely, the enjoyment of life and liberty, with the means
of acquiring and possessing property, and pursuing and obtaining
happiness and safety.*

— Virginia Declaration of Rights, 1776.

CHAPTER ONE

The Nature and Rights of Man

SOMETIME IN MAY or early June of 1775 the Fairfax Independent Company held a meeting of historic importance in Alexandria, Virginia —of importance, that is, in the history of ideas. The Company was one of those remarkable spontaneous organizations for the military defense of freedom from British oppression which were converted a short time later into the army of independence, the continental militia. The Captain of the Company was George Washington, but the founding and guiding spirit was Colonel George Mason of Gunston Hall. Speaking to a motion for the annual election of the Company's officers, Mason used the occasion to set forth in clear and forceful terms a doctrine of the rights of man which was to serve as the philosophical base of the revolution itself, and of the Republican Party as it emerged from the political struggles of the last quarter of the eighteenth century.

"We came equals into this world," said Colonel Mason, "and equals shall we go out of it. All men are by nature born equally free and independent. To protect the weaker from the injuries and insults of the stronger were societies first formed; when men entered into compacts to give up some of their natural rights, that by union and mutual assistance they might secure the rest. But they gave up no more than the nature of the thing required."[1] From this premise Mason went on to argue that long tenure in either political or military office was to be avoided by frequent recurrence to the will of the people. Anticipating Lord Acton by a hundred years, he showed with historical examples, that power corrupts by its nature, and that human nature is prone to

I

seize such opportunities to take and hold power as occasion may offer. "But when we reflect upon the insidious arts of wicked and designing men, the various and plausible pretences for continuing and increasing authority, the incautious nature of the many, and the inordinate lust of power in the few, we shall no longer be surprised that free-born man hath been enslaved, and that those very means which were contrived for his preservation have been perverted to his ruin; or, to borrow a metaphor from Holy Writ, that the kid hath been seethed in his mother's milk."[2]

George Mason was a good deal more than a self-centered planter aristocrat. Like Jefferson, Madison, or George Wythe, he was a man of learning. His mind had been formed by study of the Greek and Roman classics, ancient and modern history, and, above all, by analysis of and adherence to the developing British concept of individual liberty. He knew well enough, as did some of his listeners, that in this speech to the Fairfax Company he was paraphrasing "the Great Mr. Locke."[3] For Mason, as for many thinkers of the eighteenth-century Enlightenment, in both Europe and America, Locke's *Second Treatise of Civil Government* marked a crucial turning point in the history not only of ideas but of freedom itself. What Locke had done, as men like Mason saw it, was to convert the ancient doctrine of natural law and social contract into a rational justification for rebellion against tyranny and for the establishment of constitutional liberty under law.

To understand the full implications of Mason's Fairfax speech and of the Republican doctrines it foreshadowed, it is necessary to look behind Locke's conception of natural law and natural rights to his analysis of human nature. The famous treatise had served several important purposes. It provided philosophical justification for the "glorious" uprising of 1688 against King James the Second in order to establish the primacy of Parliament and Constitution; it answered the cogent polemics of Sir Robert Filmer's *Patriarcha* from the point of view of the English libertarians; and it struck deeply into the heart of Hobbes's argument for authoritarian government as set forth in the *Leviathan*. In this last respect Locke performed his most useful service to the American Republicans.

Hobbes had argued that man, in a state of nature, was bestial. Natural law was the law of struggle in which might would always triumph over right. Most human beings were incapable of commanding their lusts for gain and power to socially useful ends. Hence the contract upon which civil society was based intended to place power in the hands of those few who could be trusted to exercise it in the common interest. The state of nature was the state of war. Civil society was the state of peace. But peace could be maintained only so long as the power of the rulers was absolute and uncontested. In the state of nature, according to Hobbes, men are indeed equal; but their equality is measured by their liberty to participate in a life which is "solitary, poor, nasty, brutish, and short." The only means of escape—and even this is only a partial escape—is the establishment out of sheer necessity of an absolute state in which human affairs are harmonious and peaceful in proportion as they are rigidly regulated.[4]

Behind Hobbes's analysis of nature and human nature lies, of course, the dark shadow of Calvin's doctrine of human depravity based on the Judaeo-Christian myth of the Fall of Man. Hobbes's social contract is not unlike Calvin's notion of an exclusive covenant on which Puritan social theory was based. It is no accident that both the English Revolution of 1688 and the American Revolution of 1776 involved for the future, if not for the moment, a final rejection of the Puritan world-view, and that the ideas of Locke expressed the spirit of each.

Locke's method in refuting Hobbes was to take the familiar forms provided by such concepts as "state of nature," "natural law," and "social contract," and give to them a new content. His reinterpretation rested on a buried premise regarding the nature of man. This premise, which found formal expression in Locke's *Essay Concerning Human Understanding*, was that human beings are by nature neither warlike nor peaceful, neither good nor bad, but essentially neutral and subject to alternatives of development. Upon his appearance in the world a human being has no prior leaning. His character ("nature" in the Aristotelian sense) is formed only as his experience of life unfolds. His responses to his environment accumulate to form a sort of reservoir out of which come his motivations to action. As he matures, his growing self tends to interact with his environment. As he is modified, so he modifies the conditions of his life. Gradually his understanding is formed and his behavior, good or bad, becomes "rational." The "law of nature" is now seen to be governed by "reason." That which is reasonable will be effectively operative; that which defies reason will fail. Thus it is reason which enables man to discover the "law of nature," that is, the "natural" equality of all men as they come from their Creator. The equality is an equality of *right*—to life, to liberty, and to property. But the value of natural rights tends to be impaired as their realization is frustrated by endless unrestrained competition.

And so it is that reason finds escape from the failures implicit in the state of nature by the creation of civil society, in which individuals accept limitations upon some of their liberties in order to preserve the rest. Thus the informing principle of Locke's social contract is the securing of the rights to the liberties which were potentially present in the state of nature, but incapable of realization there.[5] While Hobbes had argued for the surrender of all liberty in exchange for "peace," Locke offers no such bargain. On the contrary, his conception of civil government is open to all those risks of strife and tension and anxiety which have in fact characterized the free or "open" society. With liberty, this is to say, comes precisely that responsibility which Hobbes thought could not be managed by the vast majority of human beings. For Hobbes, as for all authoritarians, liberty and order were essentially irreconcilable principles. For Locke, as for the American Republicans, the reconciliation of these principles constituted the continuing problem of free government. Power rested ultimately and permanently in the people. By frequent and periodic appeal to the people majority will would be determined, and would give its consent to government by representative agents of the majority. Through the application of its power, thus temporarily held, government would find temporary solutions to the problem of liberty and order. The minority, too, would give its consent to and abide by these temporary solutions, so long as its rights were protected and its potentiality to become a majority by persuasion was unimpeded. The character of free government would thus be dynamic and inherently restless, in contrast to the static character of authoritarian government.

The whole of the familiar theory here briefly summarized is dependent upon the notion of man as rational, yet neither good nor bad by nature. The concept of free government derives from the prior concept of possible alternatives for human behavior. The view of Locke stands at the center between the polar opposites of Hobbes, with his assumption of natural depravity, and Rousseau, with his assumption of natural benevolence. From the one premise individual or oligarchic dictatorship is a logical deduction; from the other follows the tyranny of the majority. Because he chose the empirical method and confined himself to verifiable observation, Locke was able to avoid both extremes while recognizing the equal force of the contrasting insights on which they were founded.

Behind the speech of George Mason to the Fairfax Company lay not only the words of Locke, but a strong and growing tradition of adher-

ence to the new interpretation of natural law and the rationality of human nature of which those words were the lucid expression. There is
nothing of the extremist in Mason. If his manner appears dogmatic, it is
the firmness of cautious concern for liberty and the faith to defend it
against any attack. The dignity and equality of human persons are sacred, though human weaknesses may have "fatal effects." "To restore
mankind to its native rights" is the continuing preoccupation of responsible men. "The most effectual means that human wisdom hath ever
been able to devise, is frequently appealing to the body of the people, to
those constituent members from whom authority originated, for their
approbation or dissent. Whenever this is neglected or evaded, or the free
voice of the people is suppressed or corrupted; or whenever any military
establishment or authority is not, by some certain mode of rotation, dis-
solved into and blended with that mass from which it was taken, inevitable destruction to the state follows."[6]

Thus Mason deliberately applies a whole theory of man and government to explain his view on a simple motion offered at a meeting of a
small company of citizen soldiers. But in the Fairfax Company he saw,
as it saw in itself, an expression of the revolt of reason against oppression,
of protest against the willful violation of the social contract. From the
discussion of a motion for the annual election of military officers, set
forth in terms so far-reaching, it is no very great step to Philadelphia
and the Declaration of Independence a year later. For Mason himself,
the doctrine of this speech led to the Virginia Declaration of Rights,
for the same reasons that years later he opposed the Constitution of the
United States.

II

Several hands contributed to the drafting of the Declaration of
Rights, which was adopted by the Virginia legislature on the 12th of
June, 1776. In particular Article 16, on religious freedom, has been
shown by Irving Brant to be principally the work of Madison.[7] But
George Mason was the intellectual leader of the legislature in the 1770's,
and he was the chief author of the Declaration.

The document falls readily into two sections. The first lays down
the principles of natural rights, equality, and contract, while the second
enumerates certain of the specific rights which a free government is
obliged to guarantee. These latter are taken from the British Bill of
Rights without important alteration, and include freedom of the press,

trial by jury, protection from excessive bail and cruel or unusual punishments, as well as other safeguards which later constituted the first ten amendments to the Constitution of the United States. It was the first three paragraphs, however, all written by Mason, which served to advance Republican theory in America.

As he had done in the Fairfax Company speech, Mason lays out the familiar Lockian principles that all men are "by nature equally free and independent," and that they have certain "inherent rights," of which no compact can divest them. It is the purpose—the *only* legitimate purpose—of all government to secure the common benefit and protection of a nation. The magistrates are "trustees and servants" of the people and are at all times responsible to and removable by the people. Whenever "any government shall be found inadequate or contrary to these purposes, a majority of the community hath an indubitable, unalienable and indefeasible right to reform, alter or abolish it, in such manner as shall be judged most conducive to the public weal."[8] The notion that government rests on contract thus provides a corollary right of revolution.

But Mason's thinking has not yet led him beyond Locke to the position that only a constitutional republic can adequately secure the rights of man in America. "Of all the various modes and forms of government, that is best which is capable of producing the greatest degree of happiness and safety, and is most effectively secured against the danger of maladministration." Locke, of course, was concerned to apply the theory of contract to the justification of a constitutional monarchy. The experience, under Cromwell, of a commonwealth or republican form of government had effectively persuaded most English students of politics that some form of monarchy was a necessity. In Virginia, almost a century later, Mason was concerned in the first instance with individual freedom and only secondarily with governmental forms. The point was to commit the people of the colony to a position upon which liberty and independence could be claimed as rights. This the Declaration accomplished.

But the implications of the document, as Mason well knew, were clearly republican. Whether such a republic would be aristocratic or popular depended, of course, on matters of interpretation. The Declaration did not prescribe the qualifications of magistrates. It did provide for property qualifications on the part of the electorate. But the language was deliberately vague. Article 6 held that "all men having sufficient evidence of permanent common interest with, and attachment to the community, have the right of suffrage." The Republican interpretation of this clause, offered shortly afterward by Jefferson when the laws of the state were revised to suit the new status of independence from Britain, was that *all* men *should* have "sufficient evidence" of a proprietary interest in and attachment to the community. This meant, as Jefferson saw it, that property ought to be defined in terms of very modest acreage and that such acreage should be made available to all freemen who did not already possess it.[9] While those planters who preferred government by an elite of landed wealth interpreted the property qualification as limiting the suffrage to protect themselves against the depredations of the common man, the Republicans held that individual ownership of land was the best guarantee of dignity and responsibility on the part of any citizen. It followed that property should be defined as an inclusive rather than an exclusive principle. The common men should compose the community. The ruling elite would be chosen *by* the community *from among* the community in accordance with virtue and talent. Wealth would be neutralized.

III

The formulation of republican doctrines of natural rights was not confined to Virginia's intellectual aristocracy, though it advanced more rapidly there, perhaps, than elsewhere. In Philadelphia, the seat of the Congress, many delegates were talking gingerly of applying Lockian theories of government to the situation of the American colonies, and men like Thomas Paine were agitating and popularizing in the press. Paine's *Common Sense* papers, published in the winter and spring of 1776, gave thousands of readers an elementary education in the politics of freedom. Paine, who had arrived from England less than two years earlier, had brought with him an education both literary and practical in republicanism. He had had some association in London with Franklin and other liberal thinkers. In Philadelphia he knew Dr. Rush, Franklin's younger liberal friend, and Rush's circle. Among such people "enlightened rationalism" and Lockian political theory were commonplace. The problem, as they saw it, was to convince enough people that the series of grievances suffered at the hands of Britain was sufficient to declare a breach of contract and to proclaim independence. To Paine may go the distinction of looking sooner than most others beyond liberation toward an eventual republican form of government.

In his first paper Paine set forth the familiar contract theory of government. "Society" exists before there are "governments," but in the state of nature moral virtue is inadequate to secure the natural rights and equality of men. "Here then is the origin and rise of government; namely, a mode rendered necessary by the inability of moral virtue to govern the world; here too is the design and end of government, viz., freedom and security."[10] The proper form of government, as both Mason and Jefferson had it, was "whatever *form* thereof appears most likely to ensure it [security] to us, with the least expense and greatest benefit. . . ."[11]

But Paine now moves ahead to argue not only for independence from Britain and the right to establish a government of the Americans' own choosing. In his second *Common Sense* paper he dissects the monarchical form as currently practiced and describes its derivation from primitive ignorance. He finds that corruption, oppression, and war are the recurring characteristics of monarchy and argues that only a republic could secure the liberty the colonists would gain from independence. He proceeds to offer a rough sketch of a republican government for America. Its center would be a large, popularly-chosen legislative house in which the states themselves would be sovereign equals. Such a confederation, in Congress assembled, would elect annually an executive head or President. Office would be held on the principle of rotation. Legislation would require a three-fifths majority. "He that will promote discord, under a government so equally formed as this, would have joined Lucifer in his revolt."[12]

Paine holds no particular brief for his own proposal. It is a modest and tentative suggestion. But whatever the future structure is to be there must be no doubt that it has been legally contracted. And so he proceeds to prescribe rules for the choice of delegates to a charter convention in which will be united "the two grand principles of business, *knowledge* and *power*."[13] Knowledge can be secured by having the state legislatures name a portion of the delegates from among their own number—men qualified by experience in government—while power, which derives from the people solely, is to be provided by having other delegates elected directly in fresh voting by all qualified citizens. It is worth noting that Paine says nothing here about property qualifications for the electorate. It can be safely assumed that at this time he had no principled objection to the prevailing customs and laws on this score, though later in his turbulent career he called for universal manhood suffrage regardless of property qualifications.

The extent of Paine's influence on the American public cannot, of course, be accurately measured, but it was certainly very great. His special importance for this study, however, lies not so much in his popularization of the contract theory in justification of a war of liberation from Britain, as in the republican orientation he gave to all his writing. Republicanism was not yet the central issue when the Revolution commenced, but Paine's position was so clear and effectively stated that in the years when the Republican Party was coming into being under the Constitution appeals to "Common Sense" were commonplace.

IV

The labors of the apologists for revolution culminated in the nearly unanimous acceptance by the Congress of the Declaration of Independence. Jefferson's stately and measured language gave permanent expression to the principles advocated by Paine, Mason, and others, and marked a point closer to national unity among the colonists than they were to reach again until long after the battle over the Constitution had been fought and won. The extent to which the philosophy of the Declaration was understood, either by the signers or the people in general, cannot be determined. But there is no doubt that its pivotal position became more and more firmly established as Republican sentiment crystallized in later years.

The chief force of the Declaration was to commit the Congress to the Lockian doctrines of government by contract and the right of revolution.[14] But the document made three important contributions to the development of republican theory: 1) the principle of self-determination, which has played an increasingly significant part in the formulation of American foreign policy ever since; 2) the assertion that the assumptions of Locke's system are "self-evident"; 3) the substitution of "happiness" for "property" in the familiar formula of natural rights.

Since the problem of the Americans was not the overthrow of a domestic government supposed to have violated the terms of its contract, as had been the case in Britain in 1688, but the establishment of a claim to nationhood by colonial dependents, the notion of self-determination was a logical and necessary extension of Locke's doctrine. As such it could claim general agreement and served its purpose well. But there is an essential incompatibility between self-determination as a principle and imperial ambitions, which cannot be fully accommodated in the construction of a national foreign policy. The Republicans, by adhering to the principle during their years of opposition and striving to erect their foreign policy on it as a base in the years of their ascendancy, tended to maintain the moral integrity of their republican philosophy at the expense of a permanent inner tension in American attitudes toward the other nations of the world.[15]

In holding that the truths of natural rights philosophy are self-evident, Jefferson was no doubt following the deist's analogy with Newtonian mechanics. As the laws of nature are fixed and susceptible of formulation by human reason, so the laws of man are controlled by a rational principle and similarly capable of understanding and formulation. The "truths" of society and government are not constructed by reason; they are "discovered" by it. However open Jefferson's proposition may be to scientific or logical criticism, he secured his great point for the Republicans of the future. For, by resting the claims to right and equality on faith, he removed the major premises of Republicanism from the area of theoretical dispute so conclusively that even the most cynical Federalist of later years was careful, at least in public utterance, to confine his polemics to matters of program.

In the Virginia Declaration Mason had added "pursuing and obtaining happiness" to Locke's list of the inherent rights of man. In the Declaration of Independence Jefferson omitted property altogether and placed the "pursuit of happiness" in its stead. Students of the Declaration and of the philosophy from which it emerged have differed as to the reasons both for the substitution and its acceptance by the Congress. Some have thought that happiness was understood by the signers (perhaps by Jefferson himself) to include property as defining happiness. Others have concluded that property was so universally looked upon as a natural right at stake in the struggle with Britain that its omission from the list passed without notice. Still others have assumed that the point was merely literary or rhetorical. In general there is agreement that, whatever the reason, the language of the Declaration intended no departure from the familiar concepts. It is nevertheless clear that Jefferson was himself reconsidering the whole question of property, as his proposals for the Virginia constitution show. And Madison, some years later, deliberately placed human rights above property rights in a sense which strikingly foreshadowed twentieth century attitudes as expressed by Franklin Roosevelt in the New Deal era.[16]

V

The philosophy of natural law and natural right upon which the American republicans based their theory of government was directed against tyranny in general. Specifically, the Lockian version, which the Americans followed, had been aimed at the tyranny of a monarch who attempted to govern by decree and claimed a divine right. The same version, as adapted by the American Revolutionists, was used to deny the authority of an imperial government—even if it were a constitutional government—over a colonial people who wished to be free and independent. Thus the issue was cast in the form of a struggle between freedom, as inhering in self-government, and tyranny, as inhering in an unrepresentative body ruling from the opposite side of a great ocean. Republican theory begins, this is to say, with the declaration of individual and collective rights against any arbitrary power imposed from without. The theory advances, in the hands of men like Jefferson and Madison, with the declaration of these rights against *any* tyranny,—any arbitrary power, whatsoever,—including the tyranny of a people's own past.

Stated in the form of a "self-evident" axiom, this latter principle, if not quite original in America, was uniquely American in its application. "The earth belongs always to the living generation," Jefferson wrote to Madison from Paris in September, 1789. The living, therefore, cannot be bound by the acts of the past, nor can the present legislate for the future.[17] Adherence to this notion as a kind of yardstick for the measurement of proposed laws underlay much of the domestic and foreign policy formulated by the Republicans in their years of opposition during the 1790's, as we shall see in later chapters. But something may be said here of the theoretical premises Jefferson offered and the reservations expressed by Madison.[18]

Jefferson, it should be remembered, had a rich opportunity, in the years from 1784 to 1789, to reconsider the whole philosophical basis of government. He was in close and continuous association with men like Condorcet, Lafayette, and La Rochefoucauld, while the deep rumblings of the coming French Revolution began to be heard. His own part in the earliest stage of that revolution was not insignificant. He was absorbing the ideas of the French republicans and constitutionalists at the same time that he was revaluating the American Revolution in order to apply its lessons to France. He renewed his friendship with Paine, who visited him in Paris, and discussed the French problem with him in the light of their common experience in America. It was a time for idealism and the dream of human equality.

Back in Philadelphia, meanwhile, Madison was engaged in the exacting and often pedestrian labor of holding the liberated American colonies in a United States and giving stability to their union. The making of the American Constitution was not, of course, achieved without the application of theory, and Madison's contribution on the theoretical side was substantial. But the greater part of the job was specifically political—the finding of workable compromises among individual interests and among factions. In this arduous work Madison came to his full maturity. Thus in the interchange of ideas on the basic question, whether the dead can bind the living, Jefferson was concerned above all with what was *right*; Madison was concerned with what would *work*.

"I set out on this ground," wrote Jefferson, "which I suppose to be self-evident, that the *earth belongs in usufruct to the living*; that the dead have neither powers nor rights over it."[19] The first and most obvious application of this additional "natural right" was to the laws regarding the disposal and holding of individual property. In France one of the foremost questions posed by the developing revolutionary situation was the breakdown of feudalism. Jefferson's thesis would give ample justification for the distribution of great estates among small holders or in outright gifts to the propertyless. But the origin of the idea, in Jefferson's own experience, had been back in Virginia during the American Revolution when he was engaged in revising the laws of his state. He had led the movement for the total abolition of primogeniture and the laws of entail, and he had tried as well to secure a modest property holding for all adult males on which a broad suffrage could be based. In 1776-1778 Jefferson's thinking on the whole question of property had rested at this point. He had already moved beyond most of his contemporary Virginians and asked for more profound reforms than were at that time practicable. But the conditions of revolutionary France were different, and his own role, largely as observer and counsellor, gave him leisure to pursue the implications of ancient property laws to radical conclusions. "Then, no man can, by *natural right*, oblige the lands he occupied, or the persons who succeed him in that occupation, to the payment of debts contracted by him. For if he could, he might during his own life, eat up the usufruct of the lands for several generations to come; and then the lands would belong to the dead, and not to the living, which is the reverse of our principle."[20] This was a long step beyond his proposed Virginia laws.

But the next step carried him into a new realm of thought about the nature of government and of power. For "what is true of every member of the society, individually, is true of them all collectively." Thus, just as laws regarding the inheritance or distribution of individual property were social rather than natural, and rested for their authority on the power of the state, which might be legal, that is by consent, or illegal, that is by arbitrary decree, so laws governing the property of a whole society, national income, national debt, public lands, etc., were also social. Society had no natural right to bind the future by its laws and regulations. There was no reason why the principle should be confined to matters of property. Its extent was universal. "No society can make a perpetual constitution, or even a perpetual law. The earth belongs always to the living generation: they may manage it, then, and what proceeds from it, as they please, during their usufruct. They are masters, too, of their own persons, and consequently may govern them as they please. But persons and property make the sum of the objects of government. The constitution and the laws of their predecessors are extinguished then, in their natural course, with those whose will gave them being. This could preserve that being, till it ceased to be itself, and no longer."[21]

In the first draft of his letter Jefferson had computed the life of a generation at thirty-four years. Using Buffon's tables of mortality which showed that thirty-four years was the normal expectancy of a man at the age of twenty-one, he had simply assumed a generation born on the same day and dying on the same day. In the final draft he corrected this error by striking an artificial average. This gave him nineteen years as the average life of a generation. Thus constitutional provisions, public laws, public debts, and all other exercises of state power were valid for nineteen years only. Their persistence beyond that point would depend upon assent by the new generation.

At the conclusion, Jefferson suggested that Madison not only meditate the whole thesis, but actually introduce it as preamble to the first tax law promulgated by the new government of the United States under the Constitution. "No nation can make a declaration against the validity of long-contracted debts, so disinterestedly as we, since we do not owe a shilling which will not be paid, principal and interest, by the measures you have taken, within the time of our own lives."[22] Though Madison was unable to accept Jefferson's whole development of the idea and made certain sharply constricting reservations, it nevertheless becomes clear that the Republican leaders of the next decade were already sufficiently agreed to be able to formulate a theoretical position which would place them squarely against the whole of Hamilton's program for solving the fiscal problem of the infant United States.

Madison's chief reaction, as set forth in his letter of February 4, 1790, was that "the earth belongs to the living" would be a splendid principle upon which to base "philosophical legislation," but that such legislation could not be expected from the men in power in America, or perhaps for a very long time to come. But there were two important qualifications to be made even on the philosophical plane. While it was true that the earth in its *natural state* belonged to the living generation as a *natural right*, it did not follow that the living had natural right to the *improvements* made by the dead, since these were by natural right the property of the dead. It followed that the dead hold the living under a certain obligation, and the living have a similar obligation to the future. The same principle was applicable to the contracting of debts. Certain debts are contracted for the advantage of future generations, such as those involved in basic improvements or in wars of national defense. Thus a corollary took shape. "All that seems indispensable in stating the account between the dead and the living, is to see that the debts against the latter do not exceed the advances made by the former."[23] In later years, as we shall see, the original thesis thus qualified became, in the hands of Albert Gallatin, the cornerstone of Republican fiscal policy.

The second great qualification made by Madison dealt with the problem of the maintenance of political stability if a constitution were understood to be binding by natural law no longer than nineteen years. While Jefferson had argued that each new generation would have to give a positive reaffirmation both to constitutions and statutes else their sanction in natural law would lapse, Madison preferred to state the position in more familiar negative terms. If there were no "express revocation" it was safe to assume that a new generation has given "tacit consent." Indeed, it would be necessary to assume such tacit consent, since the principle of majority rule rested on it.

> On what principle is it that the voice of the majority binds the minority? It does not result I conceive from a law of nature but from compact founded on utility. A greater proportion might be required

by the fundamental Constitution of Society, if under any particular circumstances it were judged eligible. Prior therefore to the establishment of this principle, *unanimity* was necessary; and rigid Theory, accordingly presupposes the assent of every individual to the rule, which subjects the minority to the will of the majority. If this assent cannot be given tacitly, or be not implied where no positive evidence forbids, no person born in Society, could on attaining age, be bound by any acts of the majority, and either a unanimous renewal of every law would be necessary, as often as a new member should be added to the Society, or the express consent of every new member be obtained to the rule by which the majority decides for the whole.[24]

The difference between the two men arose from their differing preoccupations. Jefferson is thinking of the individual under conditions in which he is being unjustly or unwisely governed, and searching for a grounded theory which would allow him to take measures to alleviate his circumstance. The assumption is that government is bad. Madison, on the other hand, is thinking in terms of the construction of a stable government in which justice for the individual is secured by wise constitutional measures. The assumption in this case is the need for stability and continuity. But the difference is less fundamental than it appears. Both men accept Locke's thesis that government—any government—is by contract; and both agree that unjust governments violate the natural rights of citizens and are therefore without sanction in the law of nature. As baldly stated by Jefferson, the doctrine that "the earth belongs always to the living generation" is a revolutionary slogan, appropriately applied in a revolutionary situation. As qualified by Madison, the moral value of the doctrine is retained while adjusting it for practical application to the development of laws for a justly grounded society.

Thus in the hands of Jefferson and Madison the natural rights theory was adapted to fit the needs of a systematic republican philosophy, without sacrificing the essential axioms. The thesis that the "earth belongs to the living" was a specifically republican increment which contributed greatly, a few years later, to the definition not only of Republican policy but of the Republican dream for America.

VI

We have now before us the elements which were combined to form the theory of republican government upon which the Republican opposition, during the administrations of Washington and Adams, was based, and which guided the thinking of American leadership in the period of Republican ascendancy under Jefferson, Madison, and Monroe. These elements were, in summary: 1) the belief that human nature is neither good nor bad inherently but capable of the exercise of "reason," and of continued improvement by the choice of better alternatives; 2) human beings in a state of nature have certain equal and inalienable rights simply because they are human beings; 3) governments arise by the consent of the governed, who establish by contract an authority to secure the rights which are insecure in the state of nature; 4) under the terms of the social contract citizens accept limitations upon their liberties in order to achieve a solid measure of freedom; 5) but they do not surrender their sovereignty, and have therefore always the natural right to consider void a contract which has resulted in the loss of liberties or the spread of injustice; 6) the majority, in civil society, has the right to govern, and the minority must consent so long as its rights are protected by the majority; 7) property-holding is a measure of citizen responsibility, and the right to participate in the political process may justly be dependent upon proprietorship, but property should be distributed widely enough to enable all adult males, not disqualified by character or infirmity, to be fully participating citizens; 8) just as a tyranny imposed from without has no sanction in natural law, so no government has a right to tyrannize over the future by legislating its own interest at the expense of posterity, and all constitutional provisions and public laws are to be measured by this principle; 9) the general value and sanction of any government are to be measured by the extent to which it secures equality of opportunity for individuals and protects civil rights and liberties.

The elements here listed were, in themselves, by no means the special property of those who formed the Republican Party in the 1790's. Some of them were accepted by most American leaders regardless of their party preference, and not even the most authoritarian Federalist would have denied all of them. But it was the Republicans who gathered them together and fitted them into a systematic philosophy of government and a systematic program for the United States. From Mason's pronouncements in 1775, through the documents of the Revolution, to the speculations of Jefferson and Madison in 1789 and 1790, there is a consistent development of republican philosophy. Thus it was no accident that Paine's *The Rights of Man* should have become, as it did, a virtual handbook for the Republican Party in its opposition to the Federalists.

For, in his polemics against Burke, even though he was dealing specifically with the French Revolution in 1791, Paine laid out the theoretical positions of the American Republicans with authority and finality. In doing so he adopted Jefferson's doctrine that the "earth belongs to the living" as a major premise, and his words offer the best summary of the whole basis of Republicanism:

There never did, nor never can exist a parliament, or any description of men, or any generation of men, in any country, possessed of the right or the power of binding or controlling posterity 'to the end of time,' or of commanding forever how the world shall be governed, or who shall govern it; and therefore all such clauses, acts, or declarations, by which the makers of them attempt to do what they have neither the right nor the power to do, nor the power to execute, are in themselves null and void. Every age and generation must be as free to act for itself, *in all cases*, as the ages and generations which preceded it. The vanity and presumption of governing beyond the grave is the most ridiculous and insolent of all tyrannies. Man has no property in man; neither has any generation a property in the generations which are to follow. . . . Every generation is and must be competent to all the purposes which its occasions require. It is the living and not the dead that are to be accommodated. When man ceases to be, his power and his wants cease with him; and having no longer any participation in the concerns of this world, he has no longer any authority in directing who shall be its governors, or how its government shall be organized, or how administered.[25]

NOTES

1. Kate Mason Rowland, *The Life of George Mason*, 1892, I, 430-431.
2. *Ibid.*, 431.
3. Mason's particular source was the following passage: "Men being as has been said, by nature all free, equal, and independent, no one can be put out of this estate, and subjected to the political power of another, without his own consent, which is done by agreeing with other men to join and unite into a community for their comfortable, safe, and peaceable living one amongst another, in a secure enjoyment of their properties, and a greater security against any that are not of it." (John Locke, *Treatise of Civil Government*, ed. C. L. Sherman, 1937, 63.)
4. The core of Hobbes's view is to be found in Chs. XIII-XV of *Leviathan*.
5. The relevant passages of Locke's *Treatise* are Chs. II and VII.
6. Rowland, *op. cit.*, 431.
7. Irving Brant, *James Madison*, Vol. I, 1941, pp. 242ff. The whole question of the relation between religion and Republican doctrine is reserved for separate treatment in Chapter V.

8. The text of the Virginia Declaration may be found in my *We Hold These Truths*, 1948. (2nd edition), pp. 34-36.
9. Dumas Malone, *Jefferson the Virginian*, 1948., pp. 238-239.
10. Thomas Paine, *Representative Selections*, ed., H. H. Clark, 1944, p. 6.
11. *Ibid.*, 5.
12. *Ibid.*, 31.
13. *Ibid.*, 31-32.
14. The best analysis of the philosophy of the Declaration of Independence and its relation to the Lockian tradition is still Carl Becker's *The Declaration of Independence*, 1922.
15. The direct origins of this problem are explored in Chapter IV.
16. This point is developed in Chapter III.
17. Jefferson, *Writings*, ed., P. L. Ford, 1895, V, 115.
18. This whole matter is given separate and detailed treatment in Adrienne Koch's *Jefferson and Madison*, 1950, Ch. IV.
19. *Writings*, ed. Ford, V, 116.
20. *Ibid.*,
21. *Ibid.*, 121.
22. *Ibid.* Jefferson's consistency is evidenced by a letter to John Taylor of Caroline as late as 1816: "Funding I consider as limited, rightfully, to a redemption of the debt within the lives of a majority of the generation contracting it; every generation coming equally, by the laws of the Creator of the world to the free possession of the earth He made for their subsistence, unincumbered by their predecessors, who, like them, were but tenants for life." (*Writings*, ed. Koch and Peden, 669. 28 May, 1816.)
23. Madison, *Writings*, ed. G. Hunt, 1904, V, 439.
24. *Ibid.*, 440.
25. Paine, *op. cit.*, pp. 61-62.

. . . *the United States have adopted a modification of political power, which aims at such a distribution of it as might avoid as well the evils of consolidation as the defects of federation, and obtain the advantages of both.*

— James Madison, 1835.

. . . *a bill of rights is what the people are entitled to against every government on earth, general or particular; and what no just government should refuse, or rest on inference.*

—Jefferson to Madison, 1787.

CHAPTER TWO

The Republicans and the Constitution

THE MANIFEST FAILURES of the Articles of Confederation in the 1780's, which forced American statesmen to re-think the whole problem of constitutional government, helped signally to develop republican thought. Republican leaders were nearly unanimous in their analysis of the defects of the Articles, but differed substantially as to the best forms to be substituted. Jefferson, living in France and lacking immediate experience of the weaknesses of the Articles, wished only for amendments to strengthen them. In their dependence upon the states he thought he saw the most reliable safeguards of personal liberty:

I confess, I do not go as far in the reforms thought necessary, as some of my correspondents in America; but if the convention should adopt such propositions, I shall suppose them necessary. My general plan would be, to make the States one as to everything connected with foreign nations, and several as to everything domestic. But with all the imperfections of our present government, it is without comparison the best existing, or that ever did exist. Its greatest defect is the imperfect manner in which matters of commerce have been provided for. It has been so often said, as to be generally believed, that Congress have no power by the Confederation to enforce anything; for example, contributions of money. It was not necessary to give them that power expressly; they have it by the law of nature. When two parties make a compact, there results to each a power of compelling the other to execute it. Compulsion was never so easy as in our case, where a single frigate would soon levy on the commerce of any State the deficiency of its contributions; nor more safe than in the hands of Congress, which has always shown that it would wait, as it ought to do, to the last extremities, before it would execute any of its powers which are disagreeable.[1]

21

But Madison, Mason, Monroe, and others of Jefferson's Virginia friends, as well as the great majority of Northern leaders, had been forced by events to take a much less optimistic view.

In April, 1787, Madison set down eleven objections to the Articles which, as his detailed analysis showed, could not be remedied within the existing framework:

1. Failure of the States to comply with the Constitutional requisitions.
2. Encroachments by the States on the federal authority.
3. Violations of the law of nations and of treaties.
4. Trespasses of the States on the rights of each other.
5. Want of concert in matters where common interest requires it.
6. Want of Guaranty to the States of their Constitutions and laws against internal violence.
7. Want of sanction to the laws, and of coercion in the Government of the Confederacy.
8. Want of ratification by the people of the articles of Confederation.
9. Multiplicity of laws in the several States.
10. Mutability of the laws of the States.
11. Injustice of the laws of the States.[2]

The first seven in the list accurately defined the attitude of most practical men, whose concern was rather more with getting the public business transacted, with facilitating commerce and manufacture, than with republican theories of government. While they shared these objections, the proponents of republicanism tended to place greater emphasis upon the last four, as more directly concerned with the sanction of all government in the popular will and with the rights of man.

Thus the Republicans agreed with other American leaders on the need for a new constitution, but approached the framing of such a document with specifically democratic hopes and expectations. When the great debate over ratification of the plan submitted to the states by the convention of 1787 was under way, it was precisely the question of democratic sanction in the proposed constitution which exercised the minds of the Republicans. Some were satisfied; others were not. But whether they approved or disapproved, the theoretical basis of the positions they took remained consistent. It is important to recognize, in the light of later history, that none of the Republicans took a narrow states'-rights view. They were nationalists, concerned to secure personal liberty and popular democracy in the American republic. Men like Patrick Henry and R. H. Lee, on the other hand, were guided by a parochial concern for local interests. If they made common cause with certain of the Republicans, like Mason, it was an uneasy alliance without grounding either in philosophy or purpose.

II

In the Constitutional Convention of 1787 no very serious attempt was made to advance anything but republican ideas for the structure of the new government. But the delegates differed markedly in their degree of commitment to the republican idea. Some, like Hamilton, were quite confident that a republic would not succeed in America but were willing to give it a trial. Others, like James Wilson, lacked confidence in the ability of the people to govern themselves but felt a deep obligation to see that they had a full measure of opportunity to test the Lockian premises. At least one delegate, Elbridge Gerry of Massachusetts, was so doctrinaire in his adherence to rigid democratic theory that he was incapable of compromise and could not be satisfied with any language which might adjust the factional and personal differences of the other delegates. He fought to the end for a bill of rights and, like Mason, refused his signature because none was appended. But Gerry, in the years immediately following, tended, with some oscillation, to support Hamilton's program. Not until the X Y Z affair did he become a steady Republican and eventually Vice-President under Madison. The point of view of democratic republicanism was most consistently advanced by Franklin, Wythe, who left the Convention early, and by Mason and Madison. The two latter disagreed as to the promise of the Constitution, and Mason opposed its adoption, but they did not differ either in their commitment to republican theory or hopes for the new government.

The chief criticisms of the Constitution offered by the Republicans were that it lacked a bill of rights and that the provisions for the Presidency and the Senate were not purely republican. We shall consider these as they were expressed by Mason, Jefferson, and Monroe and then see how Madison, from the same republican viewpoint, endeavored to defend the plan which was so largely the work of his own imagination and political acumen.

In a brief but trenchant paper entitled "Objections to this Constitution of Government," Mason asserted that "since there is no Declaration of Rights, and the laws of the general government being paramount to the laws and constitutions of the several States, the Declarations of Rights in the separate States are no security."[3] It followed, he thought, that since it was sanctioned only by the constitutions of the states, the people were not "secured even in the enjoyment of the benefit of the common law."[4] Jefferson entirely agreed with this view. He called attention, also, to the fact that the Constitution guaranteed trial by jury only in criminal cases. "It was hard to conclude," he wrote to Madison, "because there has been a want of uniformity among the States as to the cases triable by jury, because some have been so incautious as to dispense with this mode of trial in certain cases, therefore, the more prudent States shall be reduced to the same level of calamity. It would have been much more just," he continued, "and wise to have concluded the other way, that as most of the States had preserved with jealousy this sacred palladium of liberty, those who had wandered, should be brought back to it; and to have established general right rather than general wrong."[5] The defence of the Constitution on this score, as presented by Wilson and others, seemed to Jefferson a dangerous quibble. "I have a right to nothing, which another has a right to take away; and Congress will have a right to take away trials by jury in all civil cases. Let me add, that a bill of rights is what the people are entitled to against every government on earth, general or particular; and what no just government should refuse, or rest on inference."[6]

From the republican point of view there could be no disputing Jefferson's contention. As the Declaration of Independence had put it, the whole purpose of government was "to secure these rights," and the British Revolution, which Locke had defended in his treatise, had produced a Bill of Rights even under a monarchy. In his reply, Madison agreed with Jefferson. But, on the scene of action, the matter seemed to him a good deal more complicated. His searching analysis of the problem is worth extensive quotation:

My own opinion has always been in favor of a bill of rights; provided it be so framed as not to imply powers not meant to be included in the enumeration. At the same time I have never thought the omission a material defect, nor been anxious to supply it even by *subsequent* amendment, for any other reason than that it is anxiously desired by others. I have favored it because I supposed it might be of use, and if properly executed could not be of disservice. I have not viewed it in an important light—1. because I conceive that in a certain degree, though not in the extent argued by Mr. Wilson, the rights in question are reserved by the manner in which the federal powers are granted. 2. because there is great reason to fear that a positive declaration of some of the most essential rights could not be obtained in the requisite latitude. I am sure that the rights of conscience in particular, if submitted to public definition would be narrowed much more than they are likely ever to be by an assumed power. One of the objections in New England was that the Constitution by prohibiting religious tests, opened a door for Jews, Turks and infidels. 3. because the limited powers of the federal Government and the jealousy of the subordinate Governments, afford a security which has not existed in the case of the State Governments, and exists in no other. 4. because experience proves the inefficacy of a bill of rights on those occasions when its control is most needed. Repeated violations of these parchment barriers have been committed by overbearing majorities in every State. In Virginia I have seen the bill of rights violated in every instance where it has been opposed to a popular current. Notwithstanding the explicit provision contained in that instrument for the rights of Conscience, it is well known that a religious establishment would have taken place in that State, if the Legislative majority had found as they expected, a majority of the people in favor of the measure; and I am persuaded that if a majority of the people were now of one sect, the measure would still take place and on narrower ground than was then proposed, notwithstanding the additional obstacle which the law has since created. Wherever the real power in a Government lies, there is the danger of oppression. In our Governments the real power lies in the majority of the Community, and the invasion of private rights is chiefly to be apprehended, not from acts of Government contrary to the sense of its constituents, but from acts in which the Government is the mere instrument of the major number of the Constituents. This is a truth of great importance, but not yet sufficiently attended to; and is probably more strongly impressed on my mind by facts, and reflections suggested by them, than on yours which has contemplated abuses of power issuing from a very different quarter.[7]

There are two crucial points in this analysis. The first is Madison's well-grounded fear that a thoroughgoing declaration of rights could not have been secured at the Convention, or perhaps from the state legislatures as then constituted. This was a realistic view of the reaction which had ensued after the political idealism of the revolutionary days. By 1787 a great many men of importance in every state were deeply concerned for the security of their property against depredations they feared from granting to the people too much direct voice in government. In their view the problem was to give to the national government

enough power to protect property and to guarantee contracts. A bill
of rights seemed to many of these men to give the common man too
great a claim against the very power which was being established to
hold him back. Probably these opponents of the rights of the common
man were less than a majority. But their influence was very great, and
no feasible government could be secured without their concurrence. If,
then, a constitution were drafted in such a manner as to secure the
rights of property and leave the civil rights of individuals no worse preserved than before, the Republicans could well be content for the moment with provisions for greater efficiency and for democratic representation and control. Meanwhile, the state ratifying conventions
would be susceptible to popular pressures, and a bill of rights might be
secured, as a result, by later amendments.

The second great point in Madison's treatment of the question is his
insistence that the danger of oppression lay not in the agencies of the
government but in the popular majority. Against tyranny arising from
the mass of the people there is no effective remedy. This is not an argument against a bill of rights. Madison's implication was, rather, that the
theoretical merit or demerit of such a bill was really irrelevant unless
the people themselves were dedicated to the preservation of individual liberty. Though he might for the moment have forgotten it, as
Madison somewhat acidly pointed out, this insight was always close to
Jefferson's heart. From it derived his insistence on the primacy of popular education on the agenda of the United States.

Jefferson, for his part, reported "great satisfaction" at receiving Madison's discussion of the problem of rights. But he did not waver from his
insistence that a bill should be added to the Constitution. He added a
new argument, "the legal check which it puts into the hands of the
judiciary."[8] To each of Madison's four points he made a brief rejoin-
der: 1. While it is possible to draft a constitution so complete that a bill
of rights is unnecessary, "in a constitutive act which leaves some precious articles unnoticed, and raises implications against others, a declaration of rights becomes necessary, by way of supplement." 2. Even
though such a declaration could not have been obtained in its entirety
at the Convention, "if we cannot secure all our rights, let us secure what
we can." 3. It may be true that the federal and state governments will
act as checks against one another, but they will need a declaration of
rights as a text upon which to base their opposition. 4. It is true that a
bill of rights is sometimes inefficacious. "But though it is not absolutely

efficacious under all circumstances, it is of great potency always, and rarely inefficacious. . . . . There is a remarkable difference between the characters of the inconveniences which attend a declaration of rights, and those which attend the want of it. . . . The executive, in our governments, is not the sole, it is scarcely the principal object of my jealousy. The tyranny of the legislatures is the most formidable dread at present, and will be for many years. That of the executive will come in its turn; but it will be at a remote period."[9]

Eventually, of course, Jefferson's view prevailed, not only among the Republicans but in amending the Constitution. In fact Madison, when he introduced the bill of rights in Congress, June 8, 1789, went well beyond anything Jefferson or Mason had suggested. His proposed first amendment, intended to be prefixed to the Constitution, declared "that all power is originally vested in, and consequently derived from, the people." Going back to the Declaration of Independence, and the Virginia Declaration of Rights he then proposed to incorporate into the Constitution itself the basic Lockian doctrines:

> That government is instituted and ought to be exercised for the benefit of the people; which consists in the enjoyment of life and liberty, with the right of acquiring and using property, and generally of pursuing and obtaining happiness and safety.
> That the people have an indubitable, unalienable, and indefeasible right to reform or change their Government, whenever it be found adverse or inadequate to the purposes of its institution.[10]

The Congress, as Madison had in effect predicted, refused to adopt this amendment. The controlling argument against it was that the Declaration of Independence was itself an official expression of the United States, so that an amendment incorporating its language was unnecessary. Whether this was the reason most prominent in the minds of the Congressmen may be disputed. But it is certain that the Republicans did not think so, and it seems clear that the Declaration did not find its historic place beside the Constitution until they came to power under Jefferson's presidency. Madison's other amendments, providing guarantees of the civil rights and liberties, were, with one important exception, adopted without significant alteration. The exception was the provision that "no state shall violate the equal rights of conscience, or the freedom of the press, or the trial by jury in criminal cases."[11] The objection to this proposal was that the bills of rights in the various states were ample guarantees. This was no doubt sufficient reason at the time, for though many Republicans, like Jefferson, Madison, and Monroe, looked upon the future of slavery with foreboding, none of them could have foreseen the catastrophe which produced the Civil War and the Fourteenth Amendment.

The struggle over the first ten amendments to the Constitution not only resulted in a clear-cut victory for the proponents of republicanism, but drew them together again after their division on the question of ratification and directed their thinking and their political activity toward common purposes.

III

The objection of certain Republicans to the Senate, as proposed in the Constitution, provides insight into a different aspect of republican thinking. The best expression of this demurrer was made by James Monroe in a document which he originally intended to publish but withdrew after it was printed because he thought it too loosely drawn. It is a remarkable paper, however—the most thorough and systematic analysis of the Constitution made by any of the Republicans, excepting only Madison's *Federalist* essays. Monroe, the most successful politician and the most popular man among all the Republicans, has always been considerably obscured by the shadows of Jefferson and Madison, but he played a significant part nevertheless in Republican deliberations, and his political career nearly measures the life of the Republican Party.

Mason, in the brief analysis of the Constitution already cited, argued that the provision for the Senate was defective, from the democratic republican point of view, because it could alter money bills and originate appropriations even though the Senators were "not the representatives of the people or amenable to them."[12] But Monroe carried the objection much further. In the earlier passages of his study he had cited as the chief weakness in the Articles of Confederation that the members of Congress were not in fact legislators but diplomats negotiating with one another on behalf of sovereign states. This principle, he thought, would be carried over and perpetuated in the Constitution. "The great defect as has been already often observed in the present form, is that of its being a diplomatic corps, a government by and for states, and not in any view of it a national one. In changing it, the object should be to correct that defect in all cases whatsoever, so far as it might be practicable, which can only be done by taking the appointment of all its officers out of the hands of the states, in their legislative characters, and placing it in those of the people, or electors by them appointed for the purpose. This has been done with the members of the house of representatives, but departed from with those of the Senate. This branch will therefore be in every respect the representative of the states, dependent on and responsible for their conduct."[13] The base of this criticism is at once democratic and national. As shared by the Republicans it serves to mark them off sharply from states'-rights critics of the Constitution. It is worth observing that while many federalists, like Hamilton and John Adams, wished to imitate the British system as closely as possible, the Republicans, as here represented by Monroe, were agreeable to an upper legislative house only if it were responsible directly to the people. Yet they were true to the ancient British theory of popular control of the public purse as the most efficient check against tyranny. If, as Mason suggests, the Senate were not to be directly chosen by the people, it should have no power over public money.

Against the background of his general objection to the structure of the Senate, Monroe went on to give specific illustrations showing how such a "diplomatic corps" might betray the national interest and the general welfare by bartering for parochial advantage. He expanded Mason's point that the Senate's power in money matters would be an evil by showing how the states differed in their economic modes and interests. By their power of veto over all legislation, the Senators could frustrate the will of the people not only in matters of taxation, appropriation, and disbursement but in the general shaping of public policy. Their control over foreign relations through the approval of treaties again removed matters of the most vital concern from the reach of the people. In fact, the provision that treaties could be ratified by two-thirds of the Senators *present* rendered it possible that in practice fundamental foreign policy commitments would be made by as few as a quarter of the members. Lastly, the Senate's power to try impeachments placed a power of the greatest consequence beyond popular control. Indeed, it was possible that an official of the government who had been chosen by the people—even the President himself—might be removed from office by a body not so chosen.

The whole force of Monroe's case against the Senate may be summed up in the contention that it would not be a democratic body and hence be unsuited to a free republic. The defence offered by *The Federalist* (Nos. 62, 63, and 64) rested on the notion that a popular assembly, like the House of Representatives, would require a check upon "the impulse of sudden and violent passions," which could only be achieved by a legislative house owing its responsibility to a different and more stable source.[14] But this was not reassuring to the Republicans. They could accept the theory of a counterweight, but not if such a weight could function beyond the control of the citizens. It is again worth observing that the position of the Southern Republicans on this matter is entirely at odds with the position of men like Calhoun who, in later years, constantly appealed to the authority of Monroe and Jefferson in defense of their adherence to a states'-rights interpretation of the Constitution. It was more than a hundred years before the Seventeenth Amendment vindicated Monroe's thesis. But in perspective his view appears not only well grounded in theory but also amply supported by experience.

IV

The third principal objection of the Republicans to the proposed Constitution was that the President, in whom very great power was to be concentrated, was eligible to serve an unlimited period of time. To Jefferson, Monroe, Mason, and others this seemed to open the way for precisely the sort of monarchy which had been destroyed by the Revolution. "Their President seems a bad edition of a Polish King," Jefferson wrote to John Adams. "He may be elected from four years to four years, for life. Reason and experience prove to us, that a chief magistrate, so continuable, is in office for life." The worst implication of such a provision, Jefferson thought, was that the office of President would become in time an object of "bribery, of force, and even of foreign interference." For it would be "of great consequence to France and England, to have America governed by a Galloman or Angloman."[15] Since the President was to be commander-in-chief of the military, it seemed to Jefferson that the invitation to initiate a military dictatorship was too attractive to allow the people to feel secure in their freedom. The term of the President ought, for these reasons, to be limited. "I wish that at the end of the four years, they had made him forever ineligible a second time."[16]

Writing to Madison a few weeks later, Jefferson put the matter in still stronger language. "If once elected, and at a second or third election out-voted by one or two votes, he will pretend false votes, foul play, hold possession of the reins of government, be supported by the States voting for him, especially if they be the central ones, lying in a compact body themselves, and separating their opponents; and they will be aided by one nation in Europe, while the majority are aided by another."[17] He went on to adduce illustrations of historic failures in the system of elective monarchies, and concluded that the only way in which warfare over the Presidency could be avoided would be to limit the term to four years followed by permanent ineligibility. "No foreign power, nor domestic party, will waste their blood and money to elect a person, who must go out at the end of a short period."[18]

Jefferson several times expressed concern that no council of state was provided as a check upon the President. Mason made this point his chief ground of objection to the office. His analysis, from this point of view, is more extended and more acute than Jefferson's and deserves full quotation:

> The President of the United States has no Constitutional Council, a thing unknown in any safe and regular government. He will therefore be unsupported by proper information and advice, and will generally be directed by minions and favorites; or he will become a tool to the Senate—or a Council of State will grow out of the principal officers of the great departments; the worst and most dangerous of all ingredients for such a Council in a free country: [for they may be induced to join in any dangerous or oppressive measures, to shelter themselves, and prevent an inquiry into their own misconduct in office. Whereas, had a constitutional council been formed (as was proposed) of six members, viz.: two from the Eastern, two from the Middle, and two from the Southern States, to be appointed by vote of the States in the House of Representatives, with the same duration and rotation of office as the Senate, the executive would always have had safe and proper information and advice. . . .]"[19]

It is clear that Mason, like Jefferson, is thinking of the President as a potential monarch open to corruption and sycophancy. The primary concern of both men is for the rights and liberties of individual men, which are to be protected *against* government—any government. They could and did adduce the massive weight of historical precedent to support their view. They were keeping the spirit of the Revolution alive. But other Republicans, no less jealous of individual liberty, attacked the problem more directly in its American setting and produced more valid criticism.

It was Monroe, again, who offered the most searching analysis of the Presidency as proposed in the Constitution. Agreeing with Jefferson and Mason that there should be an arbitrary limit to the length of time any man could serve, Monroe otherwise followed a different line of attack. As he saw it, the absence of the traditional council of state was wise for America. "If this branch had been put into commission, the state spirit would have been communicated to it, and have tainted all its measures; in addition to this there would have been less responsibility."[20] Both nationalism and democracy, this is to say, will be best served by a single responsible executive. The difficulty, from the republican point of view, is not the nature of the office, according to Monroe, but the mode of election. Here his insight is truer than Jefferson's or Mason's, or even Madison's:

A departure from the strict representative line, by adding the equal vote of the senate to the number each state hath in the house of representatives, is made in the first instance; but it is still more exceptionable in other respects. If an election shall not be made, and in all probability this will often be the case, indeed the presumption is the contrary will seldom happen, a very extraordinary subsidiary mode is resorted to. Those having the five highest votes are to be ballotted for by the house of representatives, the vote to be taken by states, and one member from each giving the vote of the state. All cases that the constitution will admit of, should be considered as likely to happen some time or other. No person then I am persuaded who will make the calculation, can behold the facility by which the chair of the United States may be approached and achieved, even contrary to the wishes of the people, without equal anxiety and surprise. Let it be admitted that the temper of the times and the ardent spirit of liberty which now prevails, will guard it for the present from such easy access; but that person has profitted but little, from the faithful admonition which all history has given him, who shall conclude from thence, that this will always be the case.[21]

Thus the Presidency shares the defect of the Senate which Monroe pointed out earlier in the same paper—it is established at too great a remove from the people. This makes the close association of the two branches doubly dangerous. And so Monroe rests his case for limiting the President's service upon the provisions that the President and Senate are jointly empowered to make treaties and to make appointments of federal officers. "Contemplating, . . . the consequences of this union, the expiration of his service, should in my opinion be accompanied with a temporary disqualification."[22]

In the light of the history of the American Presidency the objections of the older revolutionaries, like Jefferson and Mason, appear to have substantially less validity than Monroe's. Actually, of course, the articles providing for the President and the mode of his election were adopted without amendment. In one hundred and sixty odd years not more than one president has been shown to have been personally corrupt, and very few cabinet members, serving as councillors of state in Mason's understanding of the term, have been found to be guilty of misconduct or to have shielded themselves against exposure. There has never been a threat of military dictatorship by a President—even when the President was himself a military man—and, with the exception of a handful of willful propagandists during the tenure of Franklin Roosevelt, the people have never been concerned that a President intended to try to hold office for life. On the other hand, the mode of election, as Monroe foresaw, has been under almost endless discussion and has never provided full satisfaction. A portion of his objection has been met by amendment, and other amendments are pending which would place the presidential election still more directly in the hands of the people. His hope for a temporary disqualification has been realized by the passage of the Twenty-second Amendment, limiting a President to two consecutive terms.

What is more important, however, than the fate of the specific Republican objections to the Presidency, is the democratic spirit in which they were offered. And there can be no question that, as in the cases of the bill of rights and the Senate, that spirit was truer to the wishes of the people than any aristocratic or monarchial tendencies which democratic republicanism feared and opposed. But those tendencies were actual enough in the early days of the Constitution, and Republican policy had always to be on guard against encroachments upon personal liberty and democratic process. Theoretical differences between a Jefferson and a Monroe became insignificant when political realities made partisanship the order of the day, and the republicans felt the need of a Republican Party.

V

Madison alone among the great Republicans was able to accept and defend the Constitution in its entirety. For this reason his crucial position requires special attention. While his friends saw in the proposed plan dangers of monarchy, on the one hand, or irresponsible aristocracy, on the other, he saw in it not only a workable compromise between men of deeply divided interests but the best hope for a democratic republic.

Madison defended the Constitution in two quite different capacities —as co-author of *The Federalist*, a long series of periodical essays directed to the attention of the delegates to the New York ratifying convention, and as a delegate to the Virginia ratifying convention. At the latter, in June, 1788, he was the acknowledged leader of the federal bloc. In this role he chose the method of direct negotiation with opposition leaders, together with many short speeches on the floor in answer to questions and to opposition statements. Throughout the whole proceeding he tended to assume that the theoretical basis of the proposed plan was well understood, and confined himself to addressing the more immediate questions regarding the special interests of Virginia. The Virginia opposition was principally cast in the form of states'-rights partisanship, hence Madison's defense deals very little with questions of republicanism. The Republican opposition of Monroe and Mason was principled and vigorous but relatively amenable to persuasion. In the end Monroe was virtually persuaded by Madison, and Mason, though not convinced, was partially reassured by Madison's agreement to a bill of rights. The final margin was very close, 89 to 79, but was nevertheless a signal victory for Madison and a remarkable example of his political skill.[23]

Madison's defense of the Constitution in *The Federalist* was of a quite different order. Here he undertook to square the general plan, as well as its most controversial features, with the general theory of republicanism. Writing to Jefferson August 10, 1788, he was careful to disclaim responsibility for the whole work or endorsement of the views of his colleagues. "*It was undertaken last fall by Jay, Hamilton, and myself. The proposal came from the two former. The execution was thrown, by the sickness of Jay, mostly on the two others. Though carried on in concert, the writers are not mutually answerable for all the ideas of each other, there being seldom time for even a perusal of the pieces by any but the writer before they were wanted at the press, and sometimes hardly by the writer himself.*"[24] It has never been possible to make positive identification of the authorship of all the *Federalist* papers, but the most important of Madison's contributions are certain enough. These are the tenth paper, on the adjustment and compromise of factional interests, and the series of six or eight beginning with number 39 which justify the Constitution in terms of republican theory as well as popular sanction.

In *Federalist No. 39* Madison addresses the problem of republicanism directly and makes his own stand positive:

The first question that offers itself is, whether the general form and aspect of the government be strictly republican. It is evident that no other form would be reconcilable with the genius of the people of America; with the fundamental principles of the Revolution; or with that honorable determination which animates every votary of freedom, to rest all our political experiments on the capacity of mankind for self-government. If the plan of the convention, therefore, be found to depart from the republican character, its advocates must abandon it as no longer defensible.[25]

Since there has been a remarkable confusion in the use of the term, republic, and many governments which are obviously properly characterized by some other name have nevertheless been called republics, Madison proceeds to define his conception. A republic may be defined, he says, "to be a government which derives all its powers directly or indirectly from the great body of the people, and is administered by persons holding their offices during pleasure, for a limited period, or during good behavior."[26] This is a definition which at once accords with Jefferson's repeated affirmations and meets, at least on theoretical grounds, the considerations advanced by men like Monroe. Hamilton himself could agree with the formulation, though he frankly had little faith in its efficacy. The exception he did take—tacitly at this time—was rather to the earlier position that "no other form would be reconcilable with the genius of the people of America." Madison, it is worth noting, not only asserts the position confidently, but attaches it, affirmatively, to the spirit of the Revolution. It was this rock, rather than any difference of definition, on which his collaboration with Hamilton was to founder in the short space of two years.

Madison's method of defending the Constitution as republican was to square it against his definition and then to match it with the constitutions of the various states. He showed, in some detail, how the provisions of the federal document were modelled upon typical features of the state structures. Thus he placed upon the opponents of the Constitution the onus of denying that their beloved states were republics. He concluded his demonstration by calling attention to two specific provisions:

Could any further proof be required of the republican complexion of this system, the most decisive one might be found in its absolute prohibition of titles of nobility, both under the federal and State governments; and in its express guaranty of the republican form to each of the latter.[27]

In the remainder of this paper, and in the numbers immediately following, Madison showed that the form of the Constitution was not only republican but a mixture of the national and federal principles. Thus the House of Representatives derived directly from the people on a popular basis and would make laws binding upon all citizens. Hence the House gave a national character to the government. But the Senate was representative of the interests of the states and so gave to the government a federal aspect. The office of the President would combine the two through the complex method of selection, in which the electors chosen by the people and the equal representation of the states figured with more or less equal prominence. The judiciary was to be national, but would not infringe upon the rights of the states because of the limitations set upon its jurisdiction. Throughout the whole argument Madison's controlling principle is the derivation of authority from the people, so that his adherence to democratic republicanism remains consistent. His differences with his Republican friends are uniformly differences as to the efficacy of specific provisions. Thus, when the force of events led him into opposition to Hamilton and the Federalists, he could align himself with Jefferson and Monroe without any recantation of the views he had expressed in his defense of the Constitution. At the same time, his decisive position in drawing the Constitution and securing its ratification became an invaluable asset to the Republican Party in its claim of devotion to the national government.

But of more enduring significance, perhaps, was Madison's discussion, in *Federalist No. 10*, of the process by which a democratic republic would carry on its business. Twentieth-century Americans who rail against self-willed pressure groups and party spirit as the bane of democracy will do well to go back to Madison's brilliant handling of the problem. They will see how one, at least, of the founding fathers exposed the illusory basis of such objections, and showed that factions are the natural expressions of freedom and the stuff out of which democracy is made.

"By a faction," Madison wrote, "I understand a number of citizens, whether amounting to a majority or minority of the whole, who are united and actuated by some common impulse of passion, or of interest, adverse to the rights of other citizens, or to the permanent and aggregate interests of the community."[28] Factions thus defined were supposed by many at the time of the adoption of the Constitution, as at the present time, to be the source of most, if not all, public misfortunes and failures in government. There was a strongly-voiced demand that the new government should somehow do away with them. Madison proceeded to the heart of the matter. "There are two methods of curing the mischiefs of faction; the one, by removing its causes; the other by controlling its effects."

If we try to remove the causes there are, again, two ways of doing it. One is by abolishing liberty itself—which is to kill the patient instead of the disease; the other is to give "to every citizen the same opinions, the same passions, and the same interests"—which is impossible. Madison goes on to show that it is precisely freedom which breeds differences of opinion and inequalities in the distribution of property, so that factions, as expressing such differences and inequalities, are ineradicable. "The latent causes of faction are thus sown in the nature of man." Some might argue that there are men above party and factional interest who could be trusted with sufficient political power to restrain the impulses of faction. This is the ground upon which the notion of the benevolent despot has always been defended. It was also a chief reason in the minds of many who thought of George Washington as the only American who could unite the country. The cry for a heroic figure, "above party," to "unite" the country has been a recurrent cry in our political history. Madison, at the outset, denied its validity categorically, quite probably with the expectations of Washington's devotees in mind:

> It is vain to say that enlightened statesmen will be able to adjust these clashing interests, and render them all subservient to the public good. Enlightened statesmen will not always be at the helm. Nor, in many cases, can such an adjustment be made at all without taking into view indirect and remote considerations, which will rarely prevail over the immediate interest which one party may find in disregarding the rights of another or the good of the whole.[29]

The conclusion, then, is inescapable. Factions cannot be removed in a free society. We are left with the sole alternative of controlling their effects.

The controlling of the effects of faction and directing them continually toward tentative solutions of public problems turns out to be the actual business of republican government:

> If a faction consists of less than a majority, relief is supplied by the republican principle, which enables the majority to defeat its sinister

views by regular vote. It may clog the administration, it may convulse the society; but it will be unable to execute and mask its violence under the forms of the Constitution.[30]

This observation covers not only the vast majority of cases which arise within the processes of democracy, in which minority interests compete with one another on a peaceable and law-abiding basis, it justifies also such protections against lawless minorities as a republic may think necessary. Thus Madison in 1787 lays out the classic ground upon which the Smith Act of 1940, providing criminal punishments for "conspiring to teach or advocate the overthrow of the government by force or violence," was found to be constitutional in 1952.

But the case is different where a faction composes a majority. If this happens, "the form of popular government . . . enables it to sacrifice to its ruling passion or interest both the public good and the rights of other citizens." Madison saw two alternatives available in logic. One remedy would be to prevent "the existence of the same passion or interest in a majority at the same time." But this would involve the abolition of liberty itself just as surely as it would in the case of minority factions. The only feasible remedy must be to render the majority "having such co-existent passion or interest . . . by their number and local situation, unable to concert and carry into effect schemes of oppression."[31] On this showing, a small popular democracy would be most prone to the tyranny of the majority—the exact opposite of Rousseau's illusory hope. Where immediate communication among members of a majority faction bent on oppression is coupled with political means, there is no effective protection for minorities. But if the scale is enlarged the difficulties of oppression become political realities. And the larger the compass of government the more difficulties will present themselves. For this reason a republic is a safer mode of government than a pure democracy. Madison's elaboration of this thesis is worth quoting in full:

. . . the greater number of citizens and extent of territory which may be brought within the compass of republican than of democratic government . . . is [the] circumstance principally which renders factious combinations less to be dreaded in the former than in the latter. The smaller the society, the fewer probably will be the distinct parties and interests, the more frequently will a majority be found of the same party; and the smaller the number of individuals composing a majority, and the smaller the compass within which they are placed, the more easily will they concert and execute their plans of oppression. Extend the sphere, and you take in a greater variety of parties and interests; you make it less probable that a majority of the whole will have a common motive to invade the rights of other citizens; or if such a common motive exists, it will be more difficult for all who feel it to discover their own strength, and to act in unison with each other. Besides other impediments, it may be remarked that, where there is a consciousness of unjust or dishonorable purposes, communication is always checked by distrust in proportion to the number whose concurrence is necessary.

Hence, it clearly appears, that the same advantage which a republic has over a democracy, in controlling the effects of faction, is enjoyed by a large over a small republic—is enjoyed by the Union over the States composing it.[32]

Thus the force of Madison's argument was that the evil effects of faction could be better controlled by the national government, in the form of a republic, than by any other means. Factions operating at the national level would be subject to obstacles inherent in the size of the nation and the scope of the government. Factions operating at state and local levels would be subject to the national influence. Factions involving only minorities could be controlled by majority rule and turned, where not downright malevolent, to public advantage by the system of continuous adjustment and compromise.

The nearly incredible improvement in the means of transportation and communication has outstripped the increase in the number of citizens and the extent of territory within the scope of the republic to such a degree that Madison might well be less confident of his position in the middle of the twentieth century than he was at the end of the eighteenth. But no other alternative compatible with freedom has yet been devised. And it is more than probable that the rapid overcoming of the obstacles to effective factionalism is offset by the growth of loyalty to a tradition now more than one hundred and sixty years established. In the light of Madison's classic argument for "big government," the current frightened cry of domination by the national government may need to be re-examined. It may turn out that the cry arises principally from representatives of factions whose failure to achieve ambitions has led them to a healthy respect for the validity of Madison's contention.

VI

The attitude of the Republicans toward the Constitution, in the years following its adoption, has always been identified with the theory of "strict construction," and, to a large extent, even with a narrow doctrine of states'-rights. There can be no doubt that the Republicans did, sometimes for highly partisan reasons, adhere to a strict construction during their years of opposition. Certain examples of this view, like the Republican attack on the Bank of the United States, will be examined later. But it is equally true that they were amenable to a loose construction when it served their conception of the national interest without threatening individual liberty, as the case of the Louisiana Purchase amply shows. However, their radical mode of attack on the Alien and Sedition Acts of 1798, to which the Southern states'-rights politicians of a later generation appealed, was of a different order.

The four Alien and Sedition Acts were passed by Congress and signed by President Adams in the spring of 1798, at the height both of Federalist political power and of danger of war with France. The Republicans bitterly opposed all of the measures, but two of them in particular seemed to them so grossly directed against civil liberty as to be literally intolerable. One was the Alien Act itself, which gave the President authority to deport at his pleasure any "dangerous alien." The other, known as the Sedition Act, provided criminal punishments for combination or conspiracy to "oppose the government, to incite riots or insurrections against the laws of Congress; or to publish false, scandalous, and malicious writings against the government, either House of Congress, or the President, with intent to bring them into contempt, to stir up sedition, or to aid or abet a foreign nation in hostile designs against the United States." The first of these was theoretically obnoxious to believers in the right of asylum, and it was personally resented by Republican leaders on the ground that it directly affected a number of their close friends, like Joseph Priestley and Thomas Cooper who were British subjects, and the philosophers Volney and du Pont who were French citizens. The second act was looked upon as a clear-cut abridgment of the freedom of the press and of the rights of conscience and freedom of opinion.

The Republican attack came in the form of declarations known as the Virginia and Kentucky Resolutions, written by Madison and Jefferson respectively, in close collaboration with each other and with trusted Republican friends.[33] It was in these Resolutions that men like John C. Calhoun claimed, in the later years of bitter controversy over protective tariffs and slavery, to find authoritative precedent for nullification and secession. A judicious examination of the documents and of Madison's many comments on their meaning will not substantiate such a claim. Madison, in fact, lived on, in full command of his intellectual powers, through the whole of the dispute between South Carolina and the federal government over nullification, between 1828 and 1834. His estimate must be taken as final.

While Jefferson's resolution, as adopted by Kentucky, contained the word *null*, which was deleted by the Virginia legislature from Madison's draft for that body, there were no other important differences, and it will suffice to consider the Virginia Resolution and Madison's interpretations of that document. The form of this resolution was that of a declaration of opinion addressed to the legislatures of the other states and inviting their concurrence. The substance was chiefly contained in the third, fifth, and seventh paragraphs, as follows:

3. That this Assembly doth explicitly and peremptorily declare that it views the powers of the Federal Government as resulting from the Compact to which the States are parties, as limited by the plain sense and intention of the instrument constituting that compact; as no further valid than they are authorized by the grants enumerated in that compact; and that, in case of a deliberate, palpable, and dangerous exercise of other powers not granted by the said compact, the States, who are parties thereto, have the right and are in duty bound to interpose for arresting the progress of the evil, and for maintaining within their respective limits the authorities, rights, and liberties appertaining to them. . . .

5. That the General Assembly doth particularly protest against the palpable and alarming infractions of the Constitution in the two late cases of the "Alien and Sedition Acts," passed at the last session of Congress; the first of which exercises a power nowhere delegated to the Federal Government and which, by uniting legislative and judicial powers to those of executive, subverts the general principles of free government, as well as the particular organization and positive provisions of the Federal Constitution; and the other of which acts exercises, in like manner, a power not delegated by the Constitution but, on the contrary, expressly and positively forbidden by one of the amendments thereto—a power which more than any other ought to produce universal alarm, because it is levelled against the right of freely examining public characters and measures, and of free communication among the people thereon, which has ever been justly deemed the only effectual guardian of every other right. . . .

7. That the good people of this Commonwealth, having ever felt and continuing to feel the most sincere affection for their brethren of the other States, the truest anxiety for establishing and perpetuating the

union of all and the most scrupulous fidelity to that Constitution, which is the pledge of mutual friendship, and the instrument of mutual happiness, the General Assembly doth solemnly appeal to the like dispositions of the other States, in confidence that they will concur with this Commonwealth in declaring, as it does hereby declare, that the acts aforesaid are unconstitutional; and that the necessary and proper measures will be taken by each for cooperating with this State, in maintaining unimpaired the authorities, rights, and liberties reserved to the States respectively, or to the people.[34]

This Resolution, adopted by the legislature December 24, 1798, must be read together with the "Address of the General Assembly to the People of the Commonwealth of Virginia," which was adopted for printing and distribution on January 24, 1799, and is also the work of Madison.

The "Address" is the first and most important of the long series of interpretations of the Resolution, and the most reliable, since it is exactly contemporary. In it Madison deals directly with the problem raised in paragraph three of the Resolution, that the powers of the federal government derive from a compact between the states. In defense of the acts of Congress it was argued that the preamble of the Constitution set forth the doctrine that all powers derive from the people considered as a whole, hence the powers are unlimited. "On the contrary," Madison argues, "it is evident that the objects for which the Constitution was formed were deemed attainable only by a particular enumeration of each power granted to the Federal Government; reserving all others to the people, or to the States. And yet it is in vain we search for any specified power embracing the right of legislation against the freedom of the press."[35] If the states had in fact surrendered their sovereignty to the federal government in accordance with such an interpretation of the preamble, Madison points out that the actual enumeration contained within the body of the instrument would have been "frivolous." But he had no conception of "states" as distinct from the citizens who compose them. He was, in fact, disturbed lest it be thought that he identified a state legislature with a "State," or intended to suggest that the legislatures were the parties to the federal compact. "Have you ever considered thoroughly," he asked Jefferson, "the distinction between the power of the *States* and that of the *Legislature*, on questions relating to the federal pact? On the supposition that the former is clearly the ultimate Judge of infractions, it does not follow that the latter is the legitimate organ, especially as a Convention was the organ by which the compact was made."[36] The point was that the power of the federal government —of any free government—derived solely from the people, but in the case of the Constitution the mode of such derivation was from the people as divided into sovereign states. It followed that the people, again acting within state organs chosen by themselves, could reassert their sovereignty over the federal government.

The Alien and Sedition Acts, as the fifth paragraph of the Resolution set forth, seemed to offer sufficient reason for such a reassertion. Madison fills out the Republican argument in his "Address." The acts are defended by Congress and the President on the ground that a war is imminent and the country is in a state of crisis. Madison's rebuttal strikes at the root of all tyranny projected upon fear:

> Exhortations to disregard domestic usurpation, until foreign danger shall have passed, is an artifice which may be forever used; because the possessors of power, who are the advocates for its extension, can ever create national embarrassments, to be successively employed to sooth the people into sleep, whilst that power is swelling, silently, secretly, and fatally. Of the same character are insinuations of a foreign influence, which seize upon a laudable enthusiasm against danger from abroad, and distort it by an unnatural application, so as to blind your eyes against danger at home.[37]

If the Congress, under cover of an emergency, can make it a criminal offense to criticize government, then all freedom of thought and expression can be destroyed. One of the chief lines of defense of the Sedition Act is itself proof of this contention. It is said that one who is accused under the sedition law is allowed to prove the charge he has made against government or a government official and for which he is cited, such proof being adequate defense within the meaning of the law. But, says Madison, "this argument will not for a moment disguise the unconstitutionality of the act, if it be recollected that opinions as well as facts are made punishable, and that the truth of an opinion is not susceptible of proof."[38] What is worse, even the precious freedom of religion is thus placed in jeopardy, a freedom in no way connected with the danger of war with France or any other aspect of the presumed crisis.

> The sacred obligations of religion flow from the due exercise of opinion, in the solemn discharge of which man is accountable to his God alone; yet under this precedent the truth of religion itself may

be ascertained, and its pretended licentiousness punished by a jury of a different creed from that held by the person accused. This law, then, commits the double sacrilege of arresting reason in her progress towards perfection, and of placing in a state of danger the free exercise of religious opinions.[39]

Thus the Alien and Sedition Acts, and their implication of a possible general suppression of opinion, seemed to the Republicans, as here represented by Madison, to provide full justification for the call to the other states to join with Virginia in declaring these acts unconstitutional. The force of the seventh paragraph, in which such a joint declaration was invited, was too startling to win the concurrence of the other states. But, in company with Kentucky's similar call, it made a powerful impact upon public opinion and upon the Federalist majority in the Congress. Only a small number of cases were ever tried under the acts, and the laws were allowed to atrophy from disuse until they expired. The clear meaning of the Republican position, as embodied in the Virginia and Kentucky Resolutions, was that the Republicans stood for liberty first and forms of government second. But at the same time, they insisted with great intellectual power and authority that liberty under the Constitution could only be subverted by perversion of that charter. Theirs was the first great American fight for civil liberty, and its success conditioned the whole future of the United States.

But in the light of the contemporary and subsequent attempts to use the precedent of the early Republicans as justification for nullification and disruption of the Union, it is important to see how Madison defended the Resolutions on patriotic and constitutional grounds. The basis of the defense is precisely the mixed character of the federal government which he had expounded in the *Federalist*. Writing to a young friend in 1830, he points out that when the origin of the Constitution is examined, "we perceive that it is neither a Federal Government created by the State Governments like the Revolutionary Congress; nor a consolidated Government (as that term is now applied,) created by the people of the U.S. as one community, and as such acting by a numerical majority of the whole. The facts of the case which must decide its true character, a character without a prototype, are that the Constitution was created by the people, but by the people as composing distinct States, and acting by a majority in each."[40] It follows that the Constitution derives from the same source of sovereignty as the state constitutions, and is therefore equally binding upon and within the states. It also follows that as a compact among the states "in their highest sovereign capacity, and constituting the people thereof one people for certain purposes, it is not revocable or alterable at the will of the States individually, as the constitution of a State is revocable at its individual will."[41] On many occasions Madison attacked the doctrine of nullification on this ground. The point he always made was that the Resolutions had carefully spoken of the states *in the plural* as the source from which the powers of government derived, and the sovereignty, therefore, which could nullify or abolish the Constitution.[42]

The same thesis controlled, in Madison's view, the question of secession. "It surely does not follow from the fact of the states, or rather the people embodied in them, having, as parties to the constitutional compact, no tribunal above them, that, in controverted meanings of the compact, a minority of the parties can rightfully decide against the majority, still less that a single party can decide against the rest, and as little that it can at will withdraw itself altogether from its compact with the rest." He goes on to look at the obverse of the proposition, namely that all other states might secede from one, and concludes that such a doctrine is scarcely palatable. [43]

However, Madison had no wish to bind one or several states to a condition of permanent oppression. In the last year of his life, in a paper called "Notes on Nullification," he systematically attacked this problem. While neither one state nor any minority of states had a constitutional right to withdraw from the Union or to disobey the laws of the national government, there is a distinction "between a constitutional right and the natural and universal right of resisting intolerable oppression."[44] That this right would have been exercised by the Republicans at the turn of the nineteenth century, had such action been necessary to the maintenance of liberty, Madison leaves no doubt. He had subscribed to Mason's assertion of the right of revolution in the Virginia Declaration of 1776 and his faith in it, at the age of eighty-four, remains unshaken. But where a free people, protected by free institutions, governs itself by the rules of majority control and minority consent there is no sufficient reason for either nullification or secession.

Thus it may be fairly asserted that the Republicans were libertarians first, nationalists second, but nationalists none the less. Where they opposed the Constitution of the United States their ground was the security of individual freedom of action and of thought. Where they defended the Constitution it was on the ground that it could and would guarantee such security. When they insisted upon a strict construction of the Constitution they did so because such a construction seemed to them necessary for the protection of liberty. "To secure these rights," remained their constant touchstone. And so they could neither narrow their view to the parochial interests of the individual states, nor broaden it to a latitude which would have swallowed up the smaller sovereignties in a single monolithic structure. At the end of his life Madison admonished his countrymen on the merits of the American system, and in doing so he spoke clearly the spirit of the old Republicans:

> Instructed by monitory lessons . . . , and by the failure of an experiment of their own (an experiment which, while it proved the frailty of mere federalism, proved also the frailties of republicanism without the control of a Federal organization), the U.S. have adopted a modification of political power, which aims at such a distribution of it as might avoid as well the evils of consolidation as the defects of federation, and obtain the advantages of both. Thus far, throughout a period of nearly half a century, the new and compound system has been successful beyond any of the forms of Government, ancient or modern, with which it may be compared; having as yet discovered no defects which do not admit remedies compatible with its vital principles and characteristic features.[45]

NOTES

1. Jefferson, *Writings,* IV, 424.
2. Madison, *Writings,* II, 361-369.
3. Rowland, *Mason,* II, 387.
4. *Ibid.*
5. Jefferson, *Writings,* IV, 476.
6. *Ibid.,* 476-477.
7. Madison, *Writings,* V, 271-272.
8. Jefferson, *Writings,* V, 81-82.
9. *Ibid.,* 83.
10. Madison, *Writings,* V, 376-377.
11. *Ibid.,* 378.
12. Rowland, *Mason,* II, 387.
13. Monroe, *Writings,* ed. S. M. Hamilton, 1898, I, 334 ff.
14. *The Federalist,* ed. E. M. Earle, 1948., 400 ff. The authorship of these papers is undetermined, but they appear from internal evidence to be the work of Hamilton.
15. Jefferson, *Works,* ed. H. A. Washington, II, 316-317.
16. *Ibid.,* 317.
17. *Ibid.,* 330.
18. *Ibid.*

19. Rowland, *Mason*, II, 388.
20. Monroe, *Writings*, I, 336.
21. *Ibid.*, 336-337.
22. *Ibid.*
23. A reasonably full record of Madison's activities at the Virginia Convention may be found in his *Writings*, Volume V, especially pp. 123-243.
24. *Writings*, V, 246. Madison placed the whole passage in italics.
25. *The Federalist, op. cit.*, 242-243.
26. *Ibid.*, 243-244.
27. *Ibid.*, 245.
28. *Ibid.*, 54.
29. *Ibid.*, 57.
30. *Ibid.*
31. *Ibid.*, 58.
32. *Ibid.*, 60-61.
33. The best work on the Alien and Sedition Acts is John C. Miller's *Crisis in Freedom*, 1951. Adrienne Koch and Harry Ammon have made a new evaluation of the Kentucky and Virginia Resolutions, in the light of recently discovered documents in "The Virginia and Kentucky Resolutions: An Episode in Jefferson's and Madison's Defense of Civil Liberties," *William and Mary Quarterly*, April, 1948., pp. 147-176.
34. Madison, *Writings*, VI, 326-331.
35. *Ibid.*, 334.
36. *Ibid.*, 328-329. Letter to Jefferson, 29 December, 1798.
37. *Ibid.*, 333.
38. *Ibid.*, 337.
39. *Ibid.*
40. *Ibid.*, IX, 373.
41. *Ibid.*
42. See for example, *Writings*, IX, 444-445, 471 ff.
43. *Writings*, IX, 497.
44. *Ibid.*, 574.
45. *Ibid.*, 606.

One of the divisions consists of those [Federalists], who from particular interest, from natural temper, or from the habits of life, are more partial to the opulent than to the other classes of society; and having debauched themselves into a persuasion that mankind are incapable of governing themselves, it follows with them, of course, that government can be carried on only by the pageantry of rank, the influence of money and emoluments, and the terror of military force. Men of those sentiments must naturally wish to point the measures of government less to the interest of the many than of a few, and less to the reason of the many than to their weakness . . .

The other division [Republicans] consists of those who believing in the doctrine that mankind are capable of governing themselves, and hating hereditary power as an insult to the reason and an outrage to the rights of man, are naturally offended at every public measure that does not appeal to the understanding and to the general interest of the community . . .

— James Madison, 1792.

CHAPTER THREE
Domestic Policy

W HEN WASHINGTON ASSUMED office in 1789, as the first President of the United States under the Constitution, it was his earnest hope that the new government would not be blemished or, perhaps, undermined by a development of party spirit. In this hope he was undoubtedly joined by a great many Americans. It was appropriate enough, but also paradoxical, that he chose Madison as one of his closest advisers. For Madison had argued with conclusive force that parties are the natural expressions of freedom. Washington had, as a matter of fact, been elected largely because a party spirit already existed, and it was thought that his great reputation and his well demonstrated ability to measure partisan claims against the public interest would enable him to guide the nation to unity in its formative stages. No man ever tried harder. But it was the inevitable irony of his administration that the very means he used should guarantee failure. By bringing Hamilton, the brilliant young leader of the new forces of finance, industry, and strong central government, into the Treasury, and Jefferson, the intellectual leader of the older republican revolutionists, into the Department of State, Washington hoped to attach the followers of both to the new government and thereby secure its success. But, as Madison had in effect foretold, the dynamics of freedom were too powerful for the skill and determination of any man to match. In less than two years Hamilton and Jefferson had proved not only politically irreconcilable but had posed the issues and taken the first steps which would create a permanent two-party system in the United States.

The story of the party battles of the years between 1789 and 1801 has been well and frequently told.[1] Our concern here is neither with political history nor with political personalities, but rather with the domestic policy projected by the young Republican Party against the background of the political philosophy we have thus far been exploring. Nor shall we attend to the details of the controversy. It is enough to see the broad outlines and general directions.

In order to re-capture the spirit of the Republicans it is necessary to discriminate three formative conditions under which it grew and flourished. The first of these was their prior commitment to a set of political ideals demanding the adoption or retention of programs which seemed best calculated to realize them: belief in the dignity of man and the will to advance his personal liberty; moderate equalitarianism translated into equality before the law, with a "rational" distribution of property and occupations; predominance of agriculture as the way of life most conducive to happiness and virtue; economy in a government free of debt; decentralization of power; strict construction of the Constitution; and maintenance of sovereignty in the people. The second condition was the rapid development, in the years immediately following the Revolution, of an emphasis on monied property and economic enterprise, accompanied by growing fear of democracy, to which the Republicans reacted. The third was the impact of the French Revolution. To these factors in the Republican equation must be added the controlling context in which Republican policies were formulated, that is to say, in opposition to the Administration and to a small Congressional majority.

In general it is safe to say that the Republicans from the beginning usually commanded a substantial popular majority. But there were large numbers who were not qualified to vote, and like all American majorities down to the present time, it was splintered and undisciplined. In many cases affiliation was based on purely local issues. In other cases persons of sharply conflicting interests joined together for a time in what seemed to them a more compelling cause. The most effective expression of the party's political strength—the liason between Virginia and New York—was a somewhat accidental and always uneasy coalition. But in spite of the fluid nature of the Republican movement—or perhaps because of it—the individual leaders at the national level were never seriously challenged, and Republican national policy can be clearly understood through their words. Thus Jefferson, in or out of office, was always recognized as "titular" leader, while the day to day direction of political activity and the formulation of positions fell upon the shoulders of Madison, in the years from 1790 to 1796, and of Albert Gallatin, from 1796 to 1801. Many other Republican stars rose and set or continued to flicker—men like John Taylor of Caroline, W. B. Giles, John Randolph of Roanoke, James Jackson, Elbridge Gerry, George Clinton, the Livingstons of New York, and Aaron Burr.[2] But Jefferson, Madison, Gallatin, and Monroe, the latter two growing in stature and controversial importance, remained the hard core of the leadership both of the opposition before 1801 and of the government after Jefferson's election.

II

The Republican Party, as an articulate faction, had its origin in the opposition of Madison and Jefferson to Hamilton's fiscal policy in 1790. But the intellectual roots of that opposition reach much farther back. As early as 1779 Madison had written an essay on money, the implications of which led him into direct conflict with Hamilton's views. And in 1785 and 1786, while Jefferson was in France, he and Madison had exchanged ideas on property and occupations which set forth the vision of an America wholly different from that which Hamilton projected.

In October, 1785, Jefferson wrote Madison at length about the paradox of poverty in the midst of potential plenty. He had been observing in France the cruel fact of unemployment while vast acreages remained uncultivated. A conversation with a poor woman, who labored by the day when she could find work, led him, he said, "into a train of reflections on that unequal division of property which occasions the numberless instances of wretchedness which I had observed in this country and is to be observed all over Europe."[3] The land of France, he had discovered, was concentrated in the ownership of a small number of families with enormous incomes. These families employed great numbers of laborers and domestics, and there were, of course, the classes of tradesmen, sailors, and artisans. But the system left a very large surplus of chronically unemployed persons. Jefferson speculated on the reasons why there should not be work for them when so much land was uncultivated. He could find no good explanation, aside from the wealth of the landowners "which places them above attention to the increase of their revenues." At any rate there was a clear-cut moral for America,— the distribution of land must approach equality, as a principle, rather than inequality. The whole passage is of great importance:

I am conscious that an equal division of property is impracticable. But the consequences of this enormous inequality producing so much misery to the bulk of mankind, legislators cannot invent too many devices for sub-dividing property, only taking care to let their sub-division go hand in hand with the natural affections of the human mind. The descent of property of every kind therefore to all the children, or to all the brothers and sisters, or other relations in equal degree is a politic measure, and a practicable one. Another means of silently lessening the unequality of property is to exempt all from tax-ation below a certain point, and to tax the higher portions of proper-ty in geometrical progression as they rise. Whenever there is in any country, uncultivated lands and unemployed poor, it is clear that the laws of property have been so far extended as to violate natural right. The earth is given as a common stock to man to labour and live on. If, for the encouragement of industry we allow it to be appropriated, we must take care that other employment be permitted to those ex-cluded from the appropriation. If we do not, the fundamental right to labor the earth returns to the unemployed.

Jefferson then turns to the application of these principles to the United States:

It is too soon in our country to say that every man who cannot find employment but who can find uncultivated land, shall be at liberty to cultivate it, paying a moderate rent, but it is not too soon to provide by every possible means that as few as possible shall be without a little portion of land. The small landholders are the most precious part of a state.

The practical implications of this analysis for Republican policy are evident and forceful. As Madison put it, "your reflections on the idle poor of Europe, form a valuable lesson to the legislators of every coun-try, and particularly of a new one."[4] The two principal methods of rectification and security would be an inheritance policy aimed at dif-fusion of property-holding and a tax policy based on ability to pay, with incentive exemptions at the lowest level. Nearly ten years earlier Jefferson had moved in this direction by advocating abolition of primo-geniture and entail in the Virginia laws. The Republicans never deserted these principles and normally judged the efficacy, as well as the moral-ity, of Federalist proposals in the light of them.

But a still more far-reaching principle of Jefferson's thinking was that the cultivation of the earth is a natural right. He proceeded on the as-sumption that this right is not surrendered in the drawing of the social contract. Hence an economic policy which tends to produce a pauper class is contrary to natural right and not to be tolerated. If "small land-holders are the most precious part of a state," it follows that economic programs intended to encourage finance, industry, and such commerce as is not directly related to agriculture must be based on false premises to the extent that they conflict with the interests of the landholder. The whole notion of industrial development would be suspect. In practice, the Republicans were never so extreme in their views as the heat of partisanship sometimes made them appear. They did not stupidly op-pose all economic measures to encourage finance and manufactures. But they did insist that industry, finance, and commerce must be the by-products, the aid and support, of agriculture.

For his part, Madison entirely agreed with Jefferson to the point of favoring legislation directed toward ever greater distribution of the land. He also agreed that the cultivation of the earth is a natural right which every citizen retains. But he was, as usual, less optimistic than Jefferson and could not be at all sure that the full and fair use of the land would solve the problems of unemployment and poverty. "I have no doubt," he said, "but that the misery of the lower classes will be found to abate wherever the Government assumes a freer aspect, and the laws favor a sub-division of property, yet I suspect that the differ-ence will not fully account for the comparative comfort of the mass of people in the United States. Our limited population has probably as large a share in producing this effect as the political advantages which distinguish us. A certain degree of misery seems inseparable from a high degree of populousness."[5] This anticipation of Malthus's views has often been noticed. But what is more important is that Madison's concern over too great an increase in population added still another principled objection to the economic program of Hamilton and the Federalists. Like Jefferson, Madison cordially disliked urban life as a matter of taste. But the concentration of population attendant upon the development of manufactures was worse than distasteful, it was a harbinger of unem-ployment and poverty. Even in its earliest form the Republican dream had no central place for an urban proletariat any more than it had for the banker and the capitalist.

Madison had a theory of the relation between money and prices which followed directly from these premises. In 1779, during the strug-gles of the old Congress to cope with economic chaos and war, he wrote, for the purpose of clarifying his own thought, a paper on the circulation of money. He published it eventually in 1792, at a time of bitter tension with the Federalists over Hamilton's program. This paper is exceedingly valuable for an understanding of the Republican Party and its domestic policy. For one thing it effectively nullifies the shallow cliché of the historians that Madison and his friends were ignorant critics of Hamilton. For another, it shows clearly why the Republicans were never susceptible to persuasion by the Federalists in merely technical argument.

Addressing himself to the problem of inflation, Madison shows that the prevailing orthodox explanation, which Hamilton insisted upon in later years—an explanation based on the writings of men like Hume and Montesquieu—involved argument in a circle and had no real bearing on the problem. This explanation, of course, was that the increase in the quantity of the circulating medium cheapened it and forced prices upward. But this was to ignore the cause of the disease by playing one symptom off against another. The root of the matter was scarcity of commodities. And the scarcity itself was caused by monopoly.

The spirit of monopoly hath affected it [the depreciation of the currency] in no other way than by creating an artificial scarcity of commodities wanted for public use, the consequence of which has been an increase of their price, and of the necessary emissions. Now it is this increase of emissions which has been shown to lengthen the supposed period of their redemption, and to foster suspicions of public credit. Monopolies destroy the natural relation between money and commodities; but it is by raising the value of the latter, not by debasing that of the former. Had our money been gold or silver, the same prevalence of monopoly would have had the same effect on prices and expenditures; but these would not have had the same effect on the value of money.[6]

Adopting this view, as they did, Madison and his fellow Republicans could never be much impressed by plans for tinkering with the currency, by reliance upon banks, or other fiscal policies which dealt, as they saw the matter, only with surfaces. They were a hard money party, certainly, but not from defective knowledge of money and credit. They stood for independent farming, for small business, and for free trade. They were opposed to monopoly, restriction, and finance capitalism. Programs to control and manage the public debt and the public credit were inherently dangerous and would need to be constantly scrutinized lest they play into the hands of the doubters of democratic potentiality. Madison summarized the position at the very beginning of

government under the Constitution. In a speech introducing a bill providing import duties, he said,

I own myself the friend to a very free system of commerce, and
hold it as a truth that commercial shackles are generally unjust, oppressive and impolitic; it is also a truth that if industry and labor are
left to take their own course, they will generally be directed to those
objects which are the most productive, and this in a more certain and
direct manner than the wisdom of the most enlightened legislature
could point out.[7]

It is in the light of such principles as these, proceeding as they do from
a broad but well-articulated general theory of man and government,
that the opposition policies of the Republican Party in the 1790's are to
be understood.

III

The need to stabilize the economy and establish the public credit was
recognized by both Federalists and Republicans. The differences arose
as to the efficacy of means and their implications for the future. Thus
when Hamilton proposed to fund the national debt, Madison, in Congress, was agreeable but objected to indiscriminate redemption of securities and to any but the most necessary taxes. If there were no dis-
crimination, (i.e. only current holders were recognized), he pointed
out that the debt of the nation would tend to be owned by a small
group of financiers and speculators, while large numbers of citizens
who had sacrificed much in the national interest would remain impover-
ished. This was the antithesis of democratic republicanism. Excise taxes
should be levied upon luxuries so that they would fall upon those best
able to pay, whereas a flat excise on, for example, whiskey would hit
farmers and small business men who were least affluent. The sale of
western lands and import duties, Madison thought, should provide sufficient revenue to discharge the public debt within a reasonable time. It
would be necessary to fund the debt, but there must be no implication
that such a funding would be perpetual.[8] "The earth," Jefferson had
said, "belongs always to the living generation." Madison put it even
more strongly, "I go on the principle that a public debt is a public curse,
and in a republican government a greater than in any other."[9]

The three principal measures in Hamilton's fiscal program were the
funding of the debt, the assumption by the federal government of the
state debts, and the establishment of a national bank. The plan was well

articulated and admirably suited to relieve the distress of the country so far as it was caused by unstable finances. Conceived in these terms the objections of the Republicans were not unsusceptible of compromise, as Madison indicated in the case of the funding proposal. But the substantial degree of success which the whole program achieved has tended to obscure the true ground of Republican opposition. In the perspective of history it is simple enough to dismiss the opposition as deficient in financial understanding. It is, as a matter of fact, not necessary to claim financial wisdom for the Republicans in order to see the force of their position. For their deep concern was much less with the technical adequacy, or even fairness, of Hamilton's ideas than with their political implications. Madison and his friends did not forget that only three years before, in the Constitutional Convention, Hamilton had argued for a hereditary executive and a hereditary upper house in the legislature. He had made his distrust of the people and of democracy plain enough. And he had made no secret of his fears that the republican experiment would be a failure. His fiscal policy was at least as much directed to political as to economic ends. Each of the measures would at once strengthen the national government at the expense of state and local power and would, as he put it, "cement the union" by attaching the interest of the wealthy to its success.

Thus the Republicans attacked the assumption of the state debts only in part because of inequities involved in the fact that some states had already paid a greater portion of their obligations than others. This difficulty could be negotiated and adjusted, as, indeed, to some extent it was. What was more important was that the plan would transfer the interest of state creditors to the national treasury and weaken the allegiance of citizens to the state governments. This seemed to the Republicans a major step away from individual control and exercise of power. Some of the Federalist legislators, however, fearing excessive migrations of their citizens to the west unless their state taxes could be reduced by the federal assumption, were prepared to allow the union to stand or fall on the decision. The eventual solution of the problem shows that the Republicans were devoted to the union and were prepared to moderate the claims of their own self-interest while adhering to their principles.

If the state debts were to be assumed the second line of defense was to see that they were paid as quickly as possible, and Madison introduced a bill for this purpose. There was also available a means of counter thrust. A decision had to be reached as to the location of the permanent national capitol. The Republicans were concerned to have it as far removed from the centers of finance as possible without being seriously inconvenient. The southern states'-righters joined them in a demand to place it on the Potomac. Jefferson brought Hamilton and Madison together, and a compromise was reached. The state debts were assumed on a basis of reasonable equity with an understanding that they would be paid off quickly, and the capitol was located near Georgetown.[10] During the entire controversy, the Republican line was clear and consistent. In the event, they lost ground, and were to lose much more. But they were learning to organize, discovering their friends, and educating their constituency.

The debate over the national bank brought a much sharper delineation of Republican policy, since it involved a fundamental question of constitutional interpretation. On this issue, again, it is important to disregard the stereotype of the historians that Jefferson and Madison did not understand banking and spoke from provincial prejudice. Whether they understood banking or not, whether they liked or disliked banks, even whether the establishment of the national bank was wise, are matters largely irrelevant to our interest here. What cannot be questioned is that the Republicans did understand the meaning of liberty and were determined that government should secure and not dissipate it.

Madison took the lead in opposing the bank bill with two cogently drawn speeches in the House on the 2nd and the 9th of February, 1791, and, after the bill was passed, Washington invited Jefferson's written opinion on its constitutionality. The arguments may be considered together. Madison began with certain reservations as to the merits of the bill, chief of which was that it created a monopoly:

> It was proper to be considered, also, that the most important of the advantages would be better obtained by several banks, properly distributed, than by a single one. The aids to commerce could only be afforded at or very near the seat of the bank. The same was true of aids to merchants in the payment of customs. Anticipations of the government would also be most convenient at the different places where the interest of the debt was to be paid. The case in America was different from that in England: the interest there was all due at one place, and the genius of the Monarchy favored the concentration of wealth and influence at the metropolis.[11]

The establishment of branches, for which the bill provided, was no solution, since monopolistic power would still obtain. The achievements of modern transportation and communication have no doubt long since obviated Madison's objections on the score of inconvenience. But the specter of monopoly and financial concentration has never ceased to plague the United States.

Whatever the practical merits of the bill, the constitutional power assumed in projecting the bank seemed to Madison and the Republicans a far more important matter. Attacking the problem from this point of view, Madison laid down the fundamental proposition that the Constitution "is not a general grant, out of which particular powers are excepted; it is a grant of particular powers only, leaving the general mass in other hands."[12] He then proceeded to offer a set of rules for correct interpretation, which are worth quoting in full:

An interpretation that destroys the very characteristic of the Government cannot be just.

Where a meaning is clear, the consequences, whatever they may be, are to be admitted—where doubtful, it is fairly triable by its consequences.

In controverted cases, the meaning of the parties to the instrument, if to be collected by reasonable evidence, is a proper guide.

Contemporary and concurrent expositions are a reasonable evidence of the meaning of the parties.

In admitting or rejecting a constructive authority, not only the degree of its incidentality to an express authority is to be regarded, but the degree of its importance also; since on this will depend the probability or improbability of its being left to construction.[13]

Applying his proposition in accordance with these rules, Madison analyzed the bill in logical order and concise detail. Power to establish a national bank must rest upon one or more of three possible enumerations: 1) power to lay taxes to pay debts, and provide for the common defence and general welfare; 2) power to borrow money on the credit of the United States; or, 3) power to pass all laws necessary and proper to carry into execution those powers. As for the first, since the bill levied no taxes the contention was that it provided for the general welfare, which should be allowed so long as it did not interfere with the rights of the states. Madison showed not only that the bank would so interfere, but that, much worse, if the principle were allowed Congress could incorporate or establish any sort of institution, "even religious societies. . . . Congress might even establish religious teachers in every parish, and pay them out of the Treasury of the United States, leaving other teachers unmolested in their functions."[14] This latter implication is particularly worth noting as evidence of the breadth of the ground upon which the Republicans stood. They were quick to examine every proposed limitation upon individual liberty for possible restrictions upon the prior freedom of the mind and conscience.

Jefferson, addressing the same point, insisted that the constitutional grant of power to provide for the general welfare could not be separated from the power to lay taxes. That is to say, the power to lay taxes was granted in order to do three things: 1) pay the debts, 2) provide for the common defense, and 3) provide for the general welfare. There was no separate grant to provide for the general welfare. To argue that there is such a grant implied "would reduce the whole instrument to a single phrase, that of instituting a Congress with power to do whatever would be good for the United States; and, as they would be the sole judges of the good or evil, it would be also a power to do whatever evil they please."[15] He supported this contention by appealing to established rules of legal construction. "It is an established rule of construction where a phrase will bear either of two meanings, to give it that which will allow some meaning to the other parts of the instrument, and not that which would render all the others useless."[16] The debate over interpretation thus initiated has never been settled, and is no doubt incapable of final settlement. Over the years more and more latitude has been taken by Congress and supported by the Supreme Court under the welfare clause, but the Republican notion that the Constitution was "intended to lace them [Congress] up straitly within the enumerated powers," has as frequently been invoked to place a temporary halt to the extension of national power. But what was at issue in 1791 was much less a matter of policy than of principle. Thus a sentimental appeal in the twentieth century to a "Jeffersonian" interpretation of the general welfare is ultimately meaningless. The point for the original Republicans was not what the general welfare in fact was, but that the Congress had not been given the power to act upon it beyond certain well defined limits. As we shall see later, they were consistent enough in adhering to their belief. When they wished to extend the power of the government to deal with the general welfare they proposed to amend the Constitution for that purpose.

Madison's next step was to show that the bank bill could not be justified under the grant of power to borrow money. "To say that the power to borrow involves a power of creating the ability, where there may be the will, to lend, is not only establishing a dangerous principle, as will be immediately shown, but is as forced a construction as to say that it involves the power of compelling the will, where there may be the ability to lend."[17] The preamble to the bill itself, to which Madison is here directly referring, called for the instituting of such means as "might be conceived to tend to give facility to the obtaining of loans." This was, indeed, a broad enough claim even by the standards of the mid-twentieth century. It shows at once the boldness and self-confidence of Hamilton and the seriousness of the financial situation. These circumstances were enough to pass the bill, establish the bank, and further enhance the reputation of the Secretary of the Treasury. But there was no escaping the logic with which Madison attacked it. "Mark the reasoning on which the validity of the bill depends!" he warned the House. "To borrow money is made the end, and the accumulation of capitals implied as the means. The accumulation of capitals is then the end, and a bank implied as the means. The bank is then the end, and a charter of incorporation, a monopoly, capital punishments, &c., implied as the means." We are thus involved in a chain of implications to which there can be no end. "If implications, thus remote and thus multiplied, can be linked together, a chain may be formed that will reach every object of legislation, every object within the whole compass of political economy."[18]

The further Madison pressed the argument the less interested he was in the immediate question as to the efficacy of a national bank. The over-riding question was the meaning of the Constitution. Precedents were to be established. Would they tend to shore up the liberties of the citizens, or weaken them? He went back to the debate over adoption to show what the intention had then been:

The defence against the charge founded on the want of a bill of rights pre-supposed, he said, that the powers not given were retained; and that those given were not to be extended by remote implications. On any other supposition, the power of Congress to abridge the freedom of the press, or the rights of conscience, &c., could not have been disproved.[19]

On this showing there could be no legitimate claim that the bank bill was constitutional under the "necessary and proper" clause. "The explanations in the State Conventions all turned on the same fundamental principle, and on the principle that the terms necessary and proper gave no additional powers to those enumerated." Citing the debates of several conventions in support of his contention, he pointed out that a number of amendments had been proposed and rejected which would in fact have given government precisely the powers here claimed. The conclusion was not to be denied:

With all this evidence of the sense in which the Constitution was understood and adopted, will it not be said, if the bill should pass, that its adoption was brought about by one set of arguments, and that it is now administered under the influence of another set?

There remained two central objections from the Republican point of view. The bill was certainly contrary both to the ideal that the "earth belongs to the living," and to the principle that economic legislation should be measured by the principle of ever greater equality. Madison addressed himself to these points in his second speech.

The bill proposed to charter the bank for a period of twenty years,—precisely the length of what Jefferson called a generation. This was well enough, in theory, but too long in practice for so young a country. But it followed that the power to charter it must be good for twenty years also, and "granting the powers on any principle is granting them *in perpetuum.*"[20] The assumption of this right "involves the assumption of every power whatever." Thus the whole principle of limited powers, exercised in legislation limited by time and extent, is defeated. The earth does not belong to the living but to the government, which becomes an institution having a life of its own. Neither the implied return to the British monarchial continuity nor the metaphysical implication of government as a constitutive being was tolerable to republicanism. The natural-rights philosopher must insist that a republic can obtain only where the people are constitutive.

Finally, Madison asserted, the bank bill is a piece of unequal class legislation. While the Republicans could readily accept those inequalities which were produced in the free and fair competition of life, they could not support the establishment or encouragement by law of unequal holdings. The most far-reaching act of legislation thus far adopted in America—the Northwest Ordinance of 1787, which was based on Jefferson's Ordinance of 1784—had considered all citizens on an equal footing. In the bank bill "the holders of six per cent securities, will derive undue advantages. Creditors at a distance, and the holders of three per cent securities, ought to be considered, as the public good is most essentially promoted by an equal attention to the interest of all."[21]

Jefferson, strongly advising Washington to veto the bank bill, included in his opinion an eloquent plea that the establishment of such a

corporation by national charter would undermine the system of juris-
prudence upon which the state laws were based and leave the citizen at
the mercy of an irresponsible national government:

> It may be said that a bank whose bills would have a currency all
> over the States, would be more convenient than one whose currency
> is limited to a single State. So it would be still more convenient that
> there should be a bank whose bills should have a currency all over
> the world. But it does not follow from this superior conveniency, that
> there exists anywhere a power to establish such a bank; or that the
> world may not go on very well without it.
>
> Can it be thought that the Constitution intended that for a shade or
> two of convenience, more or less, Congress should be authorized to
> break down the most ancient and fundamental laws of the several
> States; such as those against mortmain, the laws of alienage, the rules
> of descent, the acts of distribution, the laws of escheat and forfeiture,
> the laws of monopoly? Nothing but a necessity invincible by any
> other means can justify such a prostitution of laws, which constitute
> the pillars of our whole system of jurisprudence.[22]

History, as well as the Federalist majority, over-ruled Jefferson's estimate of the importance to be attached to convenience in money and
banking. It has, of course, often been pointed out that Gallatin, when
the Republicans were in power, found the bank a vital element in his
fiscal program and that a second bank was established in Madison's
administration. But Gallatin never questioned the philosophy or the
motives which informed the opposition of Madison and Jefferson. He
shared them fully. The Republican fear that the bank would become an
instrument for the preservation of inequalities detrimental to the welfare of the people was at least partially justified by later developments.
The destruction of the Second Bank of the United States by Jackson
and the eventual compromise embodied in the Federal Reserve System
provide some fair measure of vindication for the Republican attack of
1791. But it is worth repeating that in opposing the bank, as well as the
methods of funding and the assumption of the state debts, the Republicans were contending for something vastly more precious than any
fiscal system. They were trying to establish a conception of the free
citizen in a free republic whose dignity and liberty must be beyond the
reaches of infringement by any authority not directly instituted and
empowered by the people.

IV

By the middle of 1791 the conflict between the Republicans and the Federalists had become bitter, open, and permanent. For some time Hamilton and his party had had a paper through which their views and polemics could gain wide circulation. In October the Republicans launched an organ of their own. The *National Gazette* was edited by Philip Freneau, Madison's old friend from college days at Princeton, and was in part supported by contracts to print official papers of the Department of State. Jefferson, in addition, employed Freneau as a part-time clerk in the Department. Hamilton, for his part, subsidized the *Gazette of the United States* by contracts to print public papers of the Treasury. President Washington deplored the partisanship both of Hamilton and Jefferson and of the papers they supported. But he found it quite impossible to restrain them effectively. Madison, reiterating the theme of the *Federalist*, explained why this was so. In an article in the *National Gazette* he laid it down that "in every political society, parties are unavoidable." The point was to prevent their doing evil and, so far as possible, render them creative. He offered five means, consistent with democratic process, to achieve these ends: 1) establish political equality among all parties; 2) withhold *unnecessary* opportunities from a few to accumulate immoderate and unmerited wealth; 3) enact laws by whose "silent operation" extreme wealth is reduced toward mediocrity and extreme indigence is raised toward a state of comfort; 4) do not allow measures which favor one party or interest at the expense of another; and 5) make one party a check upon the other wherever an accommodation or compromise cannot be reached. "If this is not the language of reason," says Madison, "it is that of republicanism."[23] In all societies, he continues, parties and interests arise out of "the nature of things," so that the art of government consists in making them checks and balances against one another. But the Federalists propose to add new parties and interests which are fostered by government and do not derive from the "nature of things." They wish to create new and artificial distinctions and then to claim that these will constitute checks and balances. "This," Madison puts it, "is as little the voice of reason, as it is of republicanism."

In a paper on "The Union" Madison raised the question as to who were the real friends of the nation and the Constitution. His firmly partisan listings of negative and positive qualifications provide an excellent insight into the state of affairs as viewed by the Republicans. Those are no friends to the union who attack others as its enemies while promoting measures which divide the people; who encourage speculation and the growth of small classes of the very rich; who wish to increase the national debt and forestall its quick discharge; who wish to replace limited government by unlimited sovereignty; who encourage the development of hereditary forms of aristocracy or monarchy. In short, those are no friends to the union who "would force on the people the melancholy duty of chusing between the loss of the Union, and the loss of what the Union was meant to secure."[24]

The true friends of the Union, on the other hand, are those who are "friends to the authority of the people;" who try to foster liberty as the *end* for which the Union was formed; who wish to retain limited government; who oppose every measure that might foster hereditary forms; who fear debt and wish to discharge it as soon as possible. In short, the real friends of the Union are the republicans who insist that Republican policy is the only lasting "cement" for a republican people.[25]

Reverting to the same theme later in the year, Madison generalized the nature of the Federalist Party, as the Republicans saw it, and the virtues and principles of the Republicans themselves. The whole passage is worth quoting as a definitive statement of the issue:

One of the divisions [of parties] consists of those, who from particular interest, from natural temper, or from the habits of life, are more partial to the opulent than to the other classes of society; and having debauched themselves into a persuasion that mankind are incapable of governing themselves, it follows with them of course, that government can be carried on only by the pageantry of rank, the influence of money and emoluments, and the terror of military force. Men of those sentiments must naturally wish to point the measures of government less to the interest of the many than of a few, and less to the reason of the many than to their weakness; hoping perhaps in proportion to the ardor of their zeal, that by giving such a turn to the administration, the government itself may by degrees be narrowed into fewer hands, and approximated to an hereditary form.

The other division consists of those who, believing in the doctrine that mankind are capable of governing themselves, and hating hereditary power as an insult to the reason and an outrage to the rights of man, are naturally offended at every public measure that does not appeal to the understanding and to the general interest of the community, or that is not strictly conformable to the principles, and conducive to the preservation of republican government.[26]

The ground of such fears as Madison expressed here—and other Republicans were frequently much less moderate—was undoubtedly less extended than he supposed. Many years later, for example, Jefferson was persuaded that John Adams had never seriously wished to destroy the republic or to institute hereditary forms within it. Yet Adams, at the outset of Washington's administration, had proposed to give to the President some such title as "His Highness the President of the United States and Protector of their Liberties." And his *Discourses on Davila* had constantly implied that a free republic would be inherently unstable and that hereditary privileged classes would be necessary for strong national government.[27] Other Federalists, like Fisher Ames, were more outspoken. Hamilton himself, in a conversation with Jefferson which the latter recorded, had asserted his allegiance to the republican experiment, but had raised serious questions as to the probability of its success.[28] The relevant point, however, is not whether the Republicans were justified in their fears by actual Federalist intentions, but that they in fact had such fears and measured, therefore, all Federalist proposals in accordance both with their fears and with Republican principles.

In the winter and spring of 1791-1792, during the period following the fight over the bank, Madison wrote an extensive series of short essays in the *National Gazette* which further crystallized Republican domestic policy. These views must be understood in the context of the party warfare and the political climate it brought about.[29] But the remarkably consistent attitude of the Republicans forbids more than a moderate allowance for polemics.

Taking up Jefferson's old theme that the "small landholders are the most precious part of a state," Madison assesses the contrasting roles of the farmer and the urban worker in the new republic. "The class of citizens who provide at once their own food and their own raiment," he says, are not only the most independent and happy. "They are more: they are the best basis of public liberty, and the strongest bulwark of public safety. It follows, that the greater the proportion of this class to the whole society, the more free, the more independent, and the more happy must be the society itself."[30] Against this principle must be measured the value of occupations in manufacturing and mechanical industry. It follows that, "whatever is least favorable to vigor of body, to the faculties of the mind, or to the virtues or the utilities of life, instead of being forced or fostered by public authority, ought to be seen with regret as long as occupations more friendly to human happiness, lie vacant."[31] Thus Madison directly opposes the implication of Hamilton's *Report on Manufactures*, which not only envisioned an industrial society as the basis of a powerful nation, but argued the advantages of industry as putting to work women and children who might otherwise be parasitical on the body economic.

As for the "several professions of more elevated pretensions, the merchant, the lawyer, the physician, the philosopher, the divine," these, wrote Madison, "form a certain proportion of every civilized society, and readily adjust their numbers to its demands, and its circumstances." Since the best distribution of citizens in a republic is "that which would most favor *health, virtue, intelligence* and *competency* in the *greatest number* of citizens," as well as secure liberty and safety, Republican policy would be forced to oppose not only the concentration of wealth through banking and speculation by a privileged minority—the Republicans would object to all measures, overt or covert, which would tend to transform the economy from agricultural to industrial. High tariffs, bounties to industrial enterprise, domestic taxes favoring manufactures, and any measures restricting free trade would be anti-republican. So far as their minority status in the government would allow, the Republicans would seek to balance the budget, discharge the debt, encourage free trade, and work toward wider and more equitable distribution of the land.

The meaning to be attached to the term *property* was crucial both in the definition of Republican policy and in assessing the differences between the two parties. At least since the time of Locke, adherents of free constitutional government had assigned a central place to property. The traditional view that status in society was to be understood in relation to property holdings was gradually modified to mean that liberty was determined by property. Thus the securing of property rights became the chief purpose of the social contract itself. The right to property was a natural right, but in the state of nature it was in constant jeopardy. The laws of civil society would therefore protect the individual by protecting his property. If property were understood to mean land, merchandise, and money, it followed that the test of a government would be its stability and financial soundness, and its power to enforce contracts. There is no doubt that many Americans, in the period following the Revolution, were primarily concerned with these criteria. The securing of property tended to become more important than the forms of government. But the more democratic the forms, the greater the voice of the small holders and the propertyless, the less satisfactory the government. A good many of the Federalists, including Hamilton, grounded their distrust of the American republic in this conviction. The Republicans were no less attached to the concept and the actuality of property than the Federalists. But they were not content with the old common-law definitions. They wished not only a far more equitable distribution of the land than did the Federalists, but to redefine the whole meaning of the term.

Madison expounded the Republican position in one of his most trenchant essays in the *National Gazette*.[32] He had no quarrel with the notion that property means "land, merchandize, and money," but insisted that the term has also a "larger and juster meaning." Rightly understood property "embraces everything to which a man may attach a value and have a right; and that *which leaves to everyone else the like advantage*."

In the latter sense, a man has property in his opinions and the free communication of them.

He has a property of peculiar value in his religious opinions, and in the profession and practice dictated by them.

He has property very dear to him in the safety and liberty of his person.

He has equal property in the free use of his faculties and free choice of the objects on which to employ them.

In a word, as a man is said to have a right to his property, he may be equally said to have a property in his rights.

The problem of government then becomes the achievement of a delicate balance between power and liberty. An excess of power leaves no man safe in any of his possessions, while an excess of liberty produces the same effect.

Government is instituted to protect property of every sort; as well that which lies in the various rights of individuals, as that which the term particularly expresses. This being the end of government, that alone is a *just* government, which *impartially* secures to every man, whatever is his own.[33]

Madison's view may be taken as a gloss on the Declaration of Independence. From the Republican side, at least, the old question whether "pursuit of happiness" means more than the acquiring and enjoying of property is resolved. Looking backward from this point, it is legitimate to wonder whether Jefferson did not deliberately alter Locke's language in order to introduce a significant ambiguity. At any rate, the ambivalence of the concept of property enabled Madison to meet the Federalists on their own ground and establish criteria for a just government which they could scarcely reject without risking the loss of all popular support.

Madison now proceeds to tip the scales in favor of the intangible properties of men. While there is a natural right to land, the exercise of the right is justly controlled by society, so that it is in part dependent on positive law. But conscience, "being a natural and inalienable right," is "the most sacred of all property." Any intrusion upon conscience or refusal to protect it is a direct and indefensible breach of the social contract itself. No matter how carefully and effectively government safeguards land, merchandise, money, and contracts it is not tolerable if it permits even indirect interference by "arbitrary restrictions, exemptions, and monopolies" with the free use of faculties and free choice of occupations by any part of the citizens. Conversely, government may not discriminate against the rich in laying taxes. Property both in material things and in ideal things must stand equal before the law. Such inequalities as may be introduced must depend upon the suffrage of the majority and should in no case upset the balance of equality in rights.

Finally, Madison lays it down that "if the United States mean to obtain or deserve the full praise due to wise and just governments, they will equally respect the rights of property, and the property in rights."[34] The American republic, in short will respect the *whole* man and deal with him in the fullness of his dignity. The Republican doctrine establishes in advance, with abundant force and clarity, the position to be taken later on such matters as the alliance with the French Republic, the settlement of the western lands, and the Alien and Sedition Acts. It argues for the long future an opposition to dominance of government by "big business" or by "big labor." It foreshadows the spirit of the New Deal in the assertion of "human rights" as against the rights of property.

V

The Whiskey Rebellion of 1794 was a severe test of both Republican policy and Republican character. Madison and others had foreseen serious popular discontent as the result of excise taxes tending to discriminate among citizens. Five years earlier, in fact, Madison had warned against a flat excise on whiskey. But the tax had been levied through democratic process, and the Republicans accepted it as the law of the land. Among the farmers of Pennsylvania's western country, however, devotion to the principles of republican government began to conflict seriously with the standard of living. To them a tax on whiskey was in effect a tax on grain itself, since in order to reach a market without unreasonable transportation costs they had to convert their grain into distilled spirits. Thus the tax hit directly at their principal, often sole, means of livelihood.

The rebellious movement was short-lived. Order was restored by the influence of local men, like Albert Gallatin, before the federal troops arrived upon the scene. But a vital issue was none the less drawn. Groups of citizens had, for a time, defied the authority of the national government and refused to comply with its laws. The Federalists, under Hamilton's stimulus, made mountains of political capital out of the episode. As they saw it, the rebellion was clear evidence that mobs of people were not to be trusted, and that liberal forms and practices encouraged mobs. A powerful, unquestioned, central government was urgently needed. The preservation of order was the first duty of government, and the primacy of the public power must be asserted. The army was called out, with Hamilton at its head, to quell the insurrection and establish the prestige of the national authority.

The Republicans, for their part, were dismayed by the whole proceeding. They sympathized with the rebels as suffering under an inequitable law. But they could not and did not condone rebellious means of protest. On the other hand, they could not and did not support the harsh measures advocated by the Secretary of the Treasury and authorized by the President. "If the insurrection had not been crushed in the manner it was," wrote Madison to Monroe, "I have no doubt that a formidable attempt would have been made to establish the principle, that a standing army was necessary for enforcing the laws."[35] Caught in the crossfire of these extremes, they found it hard to stand their ground. But stand they did. And in the upshot, they improved their position. In Pennsylvania, Gallatin, the moderate among the discontented, was elected to Congress at the head of a heavily Republican delegation. The Republicans thereby gained a new voice which was to be, for all its quiet discipline, one of the mightiest in the land. In the cities, the Republican clubs grew stronger and larger. In Philadelphia, the opposition in Congress was more firmly united and still more articulate.

An enduring political issue was posed by Washington's annual message on November 19, 1794. In the course of a review of the rebellion he referred disparagingly to "certain self-created societies" which had "assumed the tone of condemnation" of the administration.[36] The newly developing Republican clubs were clearly meant. In all of the larger cities from Charleston to Boston such clubs had made their appearance, inspired in part by fraternal feeling for the French Revolution and in part to support the Republican Party at home. Their obvious sympathy with the whiskey rebels brought them under attack by the Federalist press and somewhat alarmed Federalist politicians. When Washington took oblique notice of them in his message to Congress they became the object of formal debate. The Federalists moved to include in the then conventional reply of Congress to the President an indictment of the "self-created societies," and Madison took up their cause on behalf of the Republican opposition. The motion, he thought, struck at the heart of liberty of conscience and opinion. "An action innocent in the eye of the law could not be the object of censure to a legislative body." Congress was not only mistaken in its judgment of the societies, but had no business expressing a formal opinion. If government could freely denounce a body or an idea and throw the whole prestige of the national symbol against it, free communication of ideas, and ultimately the free press, would be frustrated. It would be only a short further step to outlaw groups and pass laws abridging the freedom of speech. "If we advert," he said, "to the nature of republican government, we shall find that the censorial power is in the people over the government, and not in the government over the people."[37] The motion, under Madison's blows, failed of passage. The whole Federalist attack, in fact, backfired. Madison was able to report to Jefferson that the Republican clubs in Baltimore, Newark, New York, and Boston were holding advertised public meetings and gaining recruits.[38]

But the Whiskey Rebellion was more than an incident. It proved the final guarantee that the two parties could never be united. Republican sympathy with the French Revolution had already frightened many conservatives. The rebellion confirmed their fears. Henceforth, Republicans became "Jacobins," or "atheistical democrats." Federalist policy became more openly directed to the interest of the financial and commercial classes and more than ever devoted to the ascendance of the national authority over not only the states but individuals. Republican cooperation became for the most part impossible, and Republican policy was forced to become more and more specific. The increasing prospect of the responsibilities of power required that principles, sufficient for purposes of opposition, be translated into programs. In this exacting task Albert Gallatin became the pivotal Republican figure of the later 1790's.

VI

Gallatin, a member of the ancient aristocracy of Geneva, had broken with his Calvinist inheritance and emigrated to America at the age of nineteen, in 1780. He had tried his hand at surveying, teaching, and other occupations, until he finally settled in western Pennsylvania as a farmer and commercial entrepreneur. His success was substantial, and he had made himself expert in financial affairs. Immediately upon his arrival in the Congress he staked out the financial field for his domain and very soon became—and remained for more than a generation—the chief Republican spokesman in economic and fiscal matters. His contributions to the formulation of Republican policy during the later years of opposition were threefold: 1) his insistence upon full and accurate reporting by the Treasury; 2) the organization of the House Committee on Ways and Means; and 3) his efforts to reduce expenditures and to discharge the public debt.

Gallatin first came to Congress as a Senator in December, 1793, but lost his seat on a technicality regarding his citizenship on February 28, 1794. He returned as a member of the House at the end of the year, and remained there until his appointment as Secretary of the Treasury under Jefferson in 1801. During his brief period in the Senate he made his presence effectively felt, and there is no question that he was disqualified in political retaliation. On January 8, 1794 he offered a motion calling for specific reports from the Treasury which at once earned him the implacable hatred of the Hamiltonian Federalists and pointed toward the introduction of a standard accounting system which had been entirely lacking under Hamilton's administration. His motion made five demands upon the Treasury: 1) a statement of the actual condition of the public debt, broken down into six categories; 2) a statement of the redeemed domestic debt, under the same categories; 3) a similar statement regarding the foreign held debt; 4) an account of the uses made of foreign loans; and 5) a summary statement of receipts and expenditures for each year since the establishment of the Constitution.[39]

What is chiefly remarkable about Gallatin's motion, as Henry Adams pointed out many years ago, is not so much that it was offered as that such reports were not already available. That the question was not raised until 1794 shows clearly enough how firm a hold Hamilton had, not only over the administration but over the Congress. Hamilton, in fact, never directly replied to the Senate request, though Gallatin's motion was passed without opposition. The Secretary paid his respects to Gallatin and the Senate in a parenthetical observation in the course of a truly remarkable letter dealing with other matters. The whole passage provides an excellent insight into the state of the government and the kind of atmosphere in which the Republicans were maintaining their opposition:

> The occupations necessarily and permanently incident to the office [Secretary of the Treasury] are at least sufficient fully to occupy the time and faculties of one man. The burden is seriously increased by the numerous private cases, remnants of the late war, which every session are objects of particular reference by the two Houses of Congress. These accumulated occupations, again, have been interrupted in their due course by unexpected, desultory, and distressing calls for lengthy and complicated statements, sometimes with a view to general information, sometimes for the explanation of points which certain leading facts, witnessed by the provisions of the laws and by information previously communicated, might have explained without those statements, or which were of a nature that did not seem to have demanded a laborious, critical, and suspicious investigation, unless the officer was understood to have forfeited his title to a reasonable and common degree of confidence. Added to these things, it is known that the affairs of the country in its external relations have for some time past been so circumstanced as unavoidably to have thrown additional avocations on all the branches of the Executive Department, and that a late peculiar calamity in the city of Philadelphia [epidemic of yellow fever] has had consequences that cannot have failed to derange more or less the course of public business.[40]

In short, the Secretary was too busy to make an accounting of his administration of the public funds, and the Senate was offensive to suggest it. The sentiment with which Hamilton concluded his letter would be looked upon by a modern executive official as literally incredible: "I will only add that the consciousness of devoting myself to the public service to the utmost extent of my faculties, and to the injury of my health, is a tranquillizing consolation of which I cannot be deprived by any supposition to the contrary." What is still more remarkable is that the Federalist administrations succeeded in avoiding formal and regularized accountings to the Congress and the people until 1800. The handicap thus placed upon the opposition is obvious. But Gallatin persisted, and using such reports as the Treasury from time to time did offer, together with calculations based upon Congressional appropriations and authorizations, he constructed a theory of the American fiscal problem which eventually supplanted Hamilton's and remained standard throughout the nineteenth century. These studies he formalized in a book, *A Sketch of the Finances of the United States*, which was published in 1796, and serving as a handbook for Republican legislators, greatly facilitated their thinking about fiscal questions.

Gallatin's next step was to insist that appropriations of money for executive expenditure be specific. As a member of the House, on December 17, 1795, he moved that a committee be established "to superintend the general operations of finance."[41] The motion carried, and the Ways and Means Committee became a standing committee of the House. If the Treasury could not be forced to make a full accounting, Gallatin's position was that at the least it could be required by law to spend money according to the direction of the Congress. Thus a kind of accounting system could be imposed in advance of expenditure. With the establishment of the committee, on which both Gallatin and Madison served, the Republican position was greatly strengthened. Republicans could not control the government, but they could act as a brake upon it, and they could build up their case to be taken to the people at elections. Above all, their attack upon the Federalist handling of the national debt became much more effective.

Gallatin's approach to the problem of the debt had the direct and simple quality of genius. He offered the elementary thesis that debt is never reduced, regardless of bookkeeping procedures, when outgo exceeds income. Hamilton, on the other hand, had borrowed from William Pitt the British idea of a sinking fund, built up by annual contributions, which represented an offset to the accumulated debt. Madison and other Republicans had accepted this notion somewhat uneasily. It remained for Gallatin to show that it was a fraud. Gallatin made his point on many occasions, but perhaps most effectively in a House debate with R. G. Harper, chairman of the Ways and Means Committee, in 1800, not long before the Republicans came to power and themselves assumed responsibility for the national finances.

Harper, arguing for an increase in the military establishment to be financed by new loans, laid down the principles of Pitt, that debt can be retired by a permanent sinking fund and held under control by always providing means of reduction when new loans are undertaken. Thus, he said, "we may gather all the roses of the funding system without its thorns."[42] Gallatin demolished this claim in an incisive speech which, as Henry Adams pointed out, anticipated the analysis of Robert Hamilton, whose essay in 1813 on the British debt was accepted by the British government as decisive. The following passage gives the substance of Gallatin's argument:

> I know but one way that a nation has of paying her debts, and that is precisely the same which individuals practise. 'Spend *less* than you receive,' and you may then apply the surplus of your receipts to the discharge of your debts. But if you spend *more* than you receive, you may have recourse to sinking funds, you may modify them as you please, you may render your accounts extremely complex, you may give a scientific appearance to additions and subtractions, you must still necessarily increase your debt. If you spend more than you receive, the difference must be supplied by loans; and if out of these receipts you have set a sum apart to pay your debts, if you have so mortgaged or disposed of that sum that you cannot apply it to your useful expenditure, you must borrow so much more in order to meet your expenditure.[43]

Gallatin proceeded to apply the analysis to the debt then in question. Since the estimated revenue was nine millions and the expenditure, including the proposed loan, was to be fourteen millions, it followed that the debt would be increased by five millions. The application of two millions to the sinking fund would only reduce the revenue available for expenditure to seven millions and necessitate the borrowing of two millions more. The increase of the debt by five millions is unavoidable. "The only difference that is produced arises from the relative price you give for the old debt and rate of interest you pay for the new. At present we pay yearly a part of a domestic debt bearing six per cent interest, and of a foreign debt bearing four or five per cent interest; and we pay both of them at par. At the same time we are obliged to borrow at the rate of eight per cent. At present, therefore, that nominal sinking fund increases our debt, or at least the annual interest payable on our debt."[44]

There were two alternatives available as Gallatin saw the matter. The one was to assume the permanence and virtue of debt and continue to accumulate it. This would guarantee the continuation of high taxes and restrictions upon the standard of living and of freedom itself. The other was to reduce expenditures so far as might be consistent with safety and retire the debt as soon as possible. This plan would release, reasonably soon, the money of the taxpayers for the improvement of their own condition, or provide the Treasury with a surplus which could be applied to the benefit of the people. These options forced Gallatin immediately into the problem of national defense.

While Gallatin had not entirely shared the views of Jefferson and Madison regarding the national bank and the funding policy, he was in complete agreement on the question of defense. In 1785, while he was in Paris trying to organize a league of civilized nations to protect commerce against piracy, Jefferson had favored the establishment of a navy. But the failure of his diplomatic efforts had persuaded him that the United States should depend upon armed privateers and accept such risks as might arise from dispensing entirely with a naval establishment. The Republicans held to this view even under the threat of war with England or France during the 1790's. Their attitude toward a standing army was always unwavering. As they saw it, standing armies were a perpetual threat to the liberties of the people. They would owe their allegiance to the executive and would offer continual temptation to the executive to install military dictatorship. A free republic would defend itself, if attacked, by means of the citizen militia; and it would never wage an aggressive war. The whole history of professional armies, as they repeated in every debate, was on their side.

Gallatin, arguing from this general point of view, drew a distinction between two kinds of defense and related both to the question of the debt. In 1796, speaking against appropriations for three new frigates, he set forth the Republican position on the whole problem of the relation between debt and defense. "I am sensible," he said, "that an opinion of our strength will operate to a certain degree on other nations; but I think a real addition of strength will go farther in defending us than mere opinion. If the sums to be expended to build and maintain the frigates were applied to paying a part of our national debt, the payment would make us more respectable in the eyes of foreign nations than all the frigates we can build. To spend money unnecessarily at present will diminish our future resources, and instead of enabling us will perhaps render it more difficult for us to build a new navy some years hence."[45] There is, this is to say, a significant difference both in kind and in value between defense conceived as a military matter and defense conceived in terms of the fundamental strength and resources of a government. In the case of the former, there is legitimate doubt as to its efficacy. The United States was far removed from any potential enemy. Communication and transportation were so slow that there could be no serious threat of a surprise attack. There would always be time to call out and deploy the militia. As for our commerce, it had never had any protection except what was provided by our seamen themselves. And it had flourished more than the commerce of any other nation in the world. Only Britain had more commercial seamen. These facts, so Gallatin urged, demonstrated the adequacy of the system of privateering, and showed that we could afford, perhaps for a long time to come, to do without the luxury of a navy.

Defense in terms of economic strength was a different matter. A country without debt would command the respect of the whole world. With no foreign creditors, the United States would have an independence more secure than any then known. In the event of major hostilities, the treasury would have money immediately available for the purchase of supplies and the payment of military salaries. If there were no war, there would be no obstacle to ever increasing prosperity. But the country was young and not yet rich. It could not have both sorts of defense. A military establishment was a good deal like the sinking fund. It would provide only the illusion of strength. Actually American progress would be indefinitely retarded—and without compensating benefit.

These were "dangerous thoughts" for 1796. The decline of the French Revolution from its early glory as a humane and dignified movement toward individual liberty had disillusioned most of the solid men of affairs in America. And the aggressive attitude of France had frightened them. Paine's *The Rights of Man*, though it did little more than re-state the familiar doctrines of natural right and republicanism characteristic of the American Revolution, now seemed subversive. To maintain a sympathetic view of France struck many people as almost treason, while to argue against military defenses, in the face of the world situation the French had precipitated, was treason indeed. What was worse, Gallatin himself had a French name and spoke with a French accent. Madison, the father of the Constitution and the long-time friend of Washington, was being reviled as a "Jacobin" for accepting honorary French citizenship, and Jefferson, an open admirer of the French, had defended the French Revolution so long that in the eyes of the Federalists he could never be trusted again. Thus Gallatin seemed even more dangerous. But he spoke firmly for the whole Republican Party when he refused to yield the principles of Republican economic policy in the face of intimidation. And he laid the practical ground work for the programs to be undertaken when the Republicans came to power.

VII

Fear of France as an aggressive power and of her insidious revolutionary influence, together with the relentless and effective opposition of the Republicans, led the Federalist majority to enact the Alien and Sedition laws of 1798. We have already seen how the Republicans fought these measures on constitutional grounds. Their chief concern during the last years of the decade was necessarily with civil liberties,— a political struggle which forms one of the most dramatic episodes in American history. But aside from sharpening their interpretation of the Constitution, it brought no significant accretions to Republican policy. The practical effect of the repressive laws, so far from wrecking the Republican Party, was to strike back at their instigators and guarantee the eventual political victory of the Republicans.

Not only was public opinion brought into sympathy with the Republicans, but they gained the support of certain important and nominally independent leaders who became disillusioned by the laws against civil liberties and by the failures of President Adams's French policy. Among these Elbridge Gerry was a conspicuous figure. Gerry, who had demanded a bill of rights at the constitutional convention, had been notoriously honest but also notoriously mercurial in his political views during the years after 1789. He maintained his early friendship with Jefferson all through the party battles, though he frequently supported the administration. In 1797 he had gone to France as a part of Adams's "XYZ" mission and tried, without success, to save something from the wreckage brought about by Talleyrand's chicanery and, perhaps, his own diplomatic ineptitude. His opposition to war led to a final break with Adams, and upon his return, he reported, in effect, to Jefferson rather than to the President.

On January 26, 1799, Jefferson wrote Gerry a letter to bind up their political alliance. It is a succinct but inclusive statement of policy which may serve to summarize the position of the Republicans on the eve of their ascent to power:

I do then, with sincere zeal, wish an inviolable preservation of our present federal Constitution, according to the true sense in which it was adopted by the States, that in which it was advocated by its friends, and not that which its enemies apprehended, who therefore became its enemies; and I am opposed to the monarchising its features by the forms of its administration, with a view to conciliate a first transition to a President and Senate for life, and from that to an hereditary tenure of these offices, and thus to worm out the elective principle. I am for preserving to the States the powers not yielded by them to the Union, and to the legislature of the Union its constitutional share in the division of powers; and I am not for transferring all the powers of the States to the General Government, and all those of that government to the executive branch. I am for a government rigorously frugal and simple, applying all the possible savings of the public revenue to the discharge of the national debt; and not for a multiplication of officers and salaries merely to make partisans, and for increasing, by every device, the public debt, on the principle of its being a public blessing. I am for relying, for internal defence, on our militia solely, till actual invasion, and for such a naval force only as may protect our coasts and harbors from such depredations as we have experienced; and not for a standing army in time of peace, which may overawe the public sentiment; nor for a navy, which, by its own expenses and the eternal wars in which it will implicate us, will grind us with public burthens, and sink us under them. I am for free commerce with all nations; political connection with none; and little or no diplomatic establishment. And I am not for linking ourselves by new treaties with the quarrels of Europe; entering that field of slaughter to preserve their balance, or joining in the confederacy of kings to war against the principles of liberty. I am for freedom of religion, and against all manoeuvres to bring about a legal ascendancy of one sect over another; for freedom of the press, and against all violations of the Constitution to silence by force and not by reason the complaints or criticisms, just or unjust, of our citizens against the conduct of their agents. And I am for encouraging the progress of science in all its branches; and not for raising a hue and cry against the sacred name of philosophy; for awing the human mind by stories of raw-head and bloody bones to a distrust of its own vision, and to repose implicitly upon that of others; to go backwards instead of forwards to look for improvements; to believe that government, religion, morality, and every other science were in the highest perfection in ages of the darkest ignorance, and that nothing can ever be devised more perfect than what was established by our forefathers. To these I will add, that I was a sincere well-wisher to the success of the French revolution, and still wish it may end in the establishment of a free and well-ordered republic; but I have not been insensible under the atrocious depredations they have committed on our commerce. The first object of my heart is my own country. In that is embarked my family, my fortune, and my own existence. I have not one farthing of interest, nor one fibre of attachment out of it, nor a single motive of preference of any one nation to another, but in proportion as they are more or less friendly to us. But though deeply feeling the injuries of France, I did not think war the surest means of redressing them. I did believe, that a mission sincerely disposed to preserve peace, would obtain for us a peaceable and honorable settlement and retribution; and I shall appeal to you to say, whether this might not have been obtained, if either of your colleagues had been of the same sentiment with yourself.

These, my friend, are my principles; they are unquestionably the principles of the great body of our fellow-citizens, and I know there is not one of them which is not yours also. In truth, we never differed but on one ground, the funding system; and as, from the moment of its being adopted by the constituted authorities, I became religiously principled in the sacred discharge of it to the uttermost farthing, we are united now even on that single ground of difference.[46]

VIII

Textbook histories of the United States have, for generations, parrotted the notion that the Republicans, once in power after 1800, quickly became conservative and followed in general the lines of policy laid down by their predecessors. Yet even a cursory examination reveals the shallow nature of such a judgment. Actually, what is remarkable is the consistency of Republican policy both in and out of power. Leonard White, in his monumental studies of early American public administration, has shown that the Republicans did in fact preserve most of the forms of organization and function which the Federalists had established, and did a better than ordinary job in improving upon them.[47] But to exercise the powers of government through inherited administrative techniques, as White himself shows, is a quite different thing from carrying on inherited policies. While there is no doubt, as scholars like Paul Appleby have clearly demonstrated, that administrative techniques and processes tend to influence policy, there is no sound implication that these techniques and methods determine what major policies shall be.[48] To these considerations may be added the evident fact that the policies of an opposition are inevitably modified in certain ways by the responsibilities of power. But when such allowances have been made, the central line of Republican thinking remains clearly discernible in almost every measure of Jefferson's administrations, until the impact of the coming war with Britain forced radical changes upon the government, and permanently darkened the Republican dream.[49]

This central line was persuasively announced in Jefferson's First Inaugural Address. The party battle of the previous decade had engendered a bitterness which the passage of the subsequent years has to some extent obscured. Yet as early as 1794 there was serious talk of disunion. No less influential political leaders than Rufus King and John Taylor of Caroline had actually corresponded about possible terms of separation. Higher echelons in the leadership of the two parties had vetoed the idea, because each side preferred to hold the union together in the hope of maintaining or gaining power. But the hatred between them grew over the years, not diminished. Thus Jefferson knew whereof he spoke when he invited his fellow citizens to "reflect that having banished from our land that religious intolerance under which mankind so long bled and suffered, we have yet gained little if we countenance a political intolerance as despotic, as wicked, and capable of as bitter and bloody persecution."[50] As President, it was his duty to placate his opponents so far as was consistent with his own mandate, and to work toward public harmony. This was, of course, the theme of his Inaugural—"We are all republicans—we are all federalists." But the famous sentence is normally cited out of context. The remainder of the passage shows not only Jefferson's adherence to Republicanism, but announces the Republican policy for dealing, at least in the first instance, with doubters and connivers. He will rely squarely on the old philosophy of the nature and rights of man:

If there be any among us who would wish to dissolve this Union or to change its republican form, let them stand undisturbed as monuments of the safety with which error of opinion may be tolerated where reason is left free to combat it. I know, indeed, that some honest men fear that a republican government cannot be strong; that this government is not strong enough. But would the honest patriot, in the full tide of successful experiment, abandon a government which has so far kept us free and firm, on the theoretic and visionary fear that this government, the world's best hope, may by possibility want energy to preserve itself? I trust not. I believe this, on the contrary, the strongest government on earth. I believe it is the only one where every man, at the call of the laws, would fly to the standard of the law, and would meet invasions of the public order as his own personal concern. Sometimes it is said that man cannot be trusted with the government of himself. Can he, then, be trusted with the government of others? Or have we found angels in the form of kings to govern him? Let history answer the question.[51]

Satisfied that he, and the majority which had elected him, could already answer the question well enough, Jefferson proceeded to announce the principles of Republican administration. Twelve may be listed:

1) support of the state governments, "as the most competent administrations for our domestic concerns and the surest bulwarks against anti-republican tendencies"
2) support of the national government "as the sheet anchor of our peace at home and safety abroad"
3) reliance upon the militia at all times except during actual invasion
4) the priority of the civil over the military
5) payment of debts
6) economy in government so that taxes may be light
7) priority to agriculture, with "commerce as its handmaid"
8) "the diffusion of information and the arraignment of all abuses at the bar of public reason"
9) freedom of religion
10) freedom of the press
11) freedom of the person protected by *habeas corpus*
12) trial by jury

The juxtaposition of the first two principles provided the context in which the remainder were to be understood, while the third, fourth, fifth, sixth, and seventh, at least in the unqualified form in which they were stated, were specifically Republican and showed in what respects the new government proposed to alter the policies of the old. Thus the backward line is continuous to the origins of republican philosophy in the turmoil of the Revolution and to the policy of the Republican Party of opposition to the earlier administrations under the Constitution. It runs through the letter of Jefferson to Gerry in 1799, the fiscal analyses of Gallatin, the attacks of Madison on Hamilton's program, the principled objections to the Constitution, the practical and theoretical discussion of Madison and Jefferson in the period of the Articles of Confederation, the writings of Tom Paine, and finally the Declaration of Independence, the Virginia Declaration, and the obscure speech of George Mason to the Fairfax Company in 1775. At the same time it is a line which leads forward to the program proposed in Jefferson's first "state of the union" message to Congress, to the domestic policy of Gallatin, and to the foreign policy of Madison and Monroe.

In Jefferson's first message, December 8, 1801, there were two considerations of particular importance for domestic policy. One was the paragraphs dealing with revenue and economy. The other was his proposal for new naturalization and immigration laws. Gallatin's long and intensive studies of the fiscal problem bore fruit at the very outset. Jefferson was able to tell the Congress that easing of international tensions and frugality of administration would permit the repeal of all internal taxes—"there is reasonable ground of confidence," he wrote "that we may now safely dispense with all the internal taxes, comprehending excises, stamps, auctions, licenses, carriages, and refined sugars, to which the postage on newspapers may be added, to facilitate the progress of information, and that the remaining sources of revenue will be sufficient to provide for the support of government, to pay the interest on the public debts, and to discharge the principals in shorter periods than the laws or the general expectations had contemplated."[52] In order to realize such a hope it would be necessary to bring about a "salutary reduction" of regular expenses. But this would accord with basic Republican thought, since the general government "is charged with the external and mutual relations only of these states." The fact was, as Jefferson saw it, that the public payrolls had been padded with large numbers of unnecessary employees, many of whom had been appointed solely for purposes of consolidating the hold of the Federalists on national power. In practice, of course, the Republicans by no means abolished the system of political appointments; and Jefferson himself ran almost immediately into the problem of meeting the claims of deserving party members. But very substantial savings were in fact made, commitments were reduced, and the internal taxes were gradually dropped. It looked as though the earth might at last truly belong to the living generation.

The Republicans had always looked upon the American democracy as a refuge for persons oppressed by tyranny. In the earlier years after the Revolution immigration and naturalization had been relatively easy, since all parties favored increasing the population. But the party struggle and the impact of the French Revolution had altered the position. The Federalist policy was increasingly restrictive until the Alien Laws were adopted in 1798. Battle on the issue was joined in Congress as early as 1794. In December of that year, after the Whiskey Rebellion at home and the abolition of titles and distinctions in France, Madison proposed new terms of naturalization which would require only three years' notice of intention and five years' residence. Giles amended the bill to require the renunciation of titles of nobility. The controversy was heated, but the Republicans carried the measure.[53] Thereafter they steadily lost ground.

In 1801 the Alien Acts expired and Jefferson proposed a new policy. Existing naturalization laws required fourteen years of residence, which was much too long in view of the mortality tables. But more important, free republicanism meant free entry and free citizenship. "And shall we refuse the unhappy fugitives from distress that hospitality which the savages of the wilderness extended to our fathers arriving in this land? Shall oppressed humanity find no asylum on this globe?"[54] While it was proper to safeguard the high offices of government by constitutional provisions of longer residence, Jefferson thought that an honest declaration of intention and fidelity was sufficient for admission to citizenship. This was an extreme view, perhaps, and no Congress has ever been quite so liberal. But the principle was accepted and continued to inform American policy for more than a hundred years. One cannot help observing that Jefferson's heart would have been stirred by the words of a writer addressing the same problem in 1953:

> The prettiest program in the world does not bear the name and address of one country, one government, one philosopher, or one sect; it is the program that is held steadily in the hearts of all people: freedom, peace, justice, light, for all and the same for all. Our own country is merely the best equipped to push it along, because of size and experience, and because we once put up a sign in the harbor saying "Send these, the homeless, tempest-tost to me . . .", and because we meant it, and because they came.[55]

IX

One vital addition to Republican domestic policy remains to be noticed—the program for internal improvements. The Republicans had always favored the development of the whole country for the benefit of agriculture and commerce, but, adhering to the principle of equal treatment of all citizens and the bending of the economy toward equality, they had opposed the partial program of the Federalists. The latter had concentrated public expenditures on military installations and the improvement of harbors. It was a policy which favored manufacturers and the merchants of the eastern seaboard. The Republicans opposed it, also, because of their commitment to the prior discharge of the debt, and their belief that constitutional authority was lacking for such federal undertakings. But by 1805 conditions enabled them to strike out for a "bold new program."

In his Second Inaugural Jefferson announced the new policy. It had been possible to dispense with internal taxes by "the suppression of unnecessary offices [and] of useless establishments and expenses . . . it may be the pleasure and pride of an American to ask, what farmer, what mechanic, what laborer, ever sees a tax-gatherer of the United States?" But the remaining revenue, on the consumption of imports, sufficed to pay the running expenses of the government, service the debt, and retire it rapidly. Very soon there would be a growing surplus, so long as commerce flourished and population grew. Jefferson now proposed that this surplus, "by a just repartition among the states, and a corresponding amendment to the Constitution, be applied, *in time of peace,* to rivers, canals, roads, arts, manufactures, education, and other great objects within each state."[56] The next sentence must sound to twentieth century ears like a quotation from some utopian fiction: "*In time of war,* if injustice, by ourselves or others, must sometimes produce war, increased as the same revenue will be increased by population and consumption, and aided by other resources reserved for that crisis, it may meet within the year all the expenses of the year, without encroaching on the rights of future generations, by burdening them with the debts of the past."

While Jefferson, returning to the same theme in his annual message of 1806, urged upon Congress and the states the enactment of appropriate amendments to the Constitution, Gallatin prepared the Republican plans.[57] These he embodied in a report of 1808 in response to a Senate resolution of 1807.

The plans called for the development of two north-south routes, four east-west systems, and connecting links between New England and the west. To connect Boston with St. Mary's in Georgia four canals would be needed—from Boston to Buzzard's Bay, from the Raritan to the Delaware, the Delaware to Chesapeake Bay, and from the Chesapeake through the Dismal Swamp, Albemarle Sound, and Pamlico Sound. The other north-south route would be a highway from Maine to Georgia involving many new links and improvements, but relying largely on already extant roads. The plan to connect east and west called for utilizing four pairs of rivers with new roads crossing mountain ranges to join each pair: the Susquehanna and the Allegheny, the Potomac and the Monongahela, the James and the Kanawha, and the Santee and the Tennessee. New England and New York were to be joined with the west by use of the Hudson and Mohawk rivers with a canal from the Hudson to Lake Ontario and another from Lake Champlain to the Hudson. There would be short canals and roads of advantage to particular localities, partly proposed to secure political support for the broader plans. The total cost was estimated at about twenty million dollars.

The whole plan was technically practicable and well within the projected income of the federal government. The war of 1812 and the constitutional question prevented its ever being carried out, except for a few minor parts. Only the National Highway (Cumberland Road) was constructed as a monument to the Republican policy of internal improvements, and it was Gallatin, again, who found a constitutional device which made it possible. This was to annex to the conditions for the admission of Ohio, in 1802, provisions for spending a percentage from the sale of Ohio's public lands to finance the building of roads connecting the state, through suitable waterways, with the Atlantic coast.

The same obstacles which prevented the realization of the policy of physical improvement of the country frustrated Jefferson's intention to spend public surpluses for the advancement of education and the arts, and he had to be content with what he could accomplish, in his old age, in his home state of Virginia. But the concept of internal improvements, physical and cultural, was an integral part of the Republicans' domestic policy, and a fitting capstone for the peaceful, prosperous, and free republic of which they dreamed. They were, despite superficial appearances, the original democratic planners, for whom the "general welfare" was indeed the welfare of the general public. Their vision was scarcely matched, in the following years, until such planning as the Tennessee Valley Authority more than a century and a quarter later. In fact, it is perhaps one of those "ironies of American history," of which Reinhold Niebuhr has written, that Gallatin and Jefferson have not long since displaced Hamilton as the better prophets of the American future.

NOTES

1. It is worth adding that no such history is entirely reliable. The issues which divided the country during its formative period still divide it, and no historian has succeeded in immunizing himself from the contagion of partisan values. But whatever preconceptions a reader of our day carries with him he will find an examination of the original records a rewarding experience.
2. The recent revival of interest in Taylor is to be applauded, but it has resulted in some grotesque historical judgments. The statement, for example, by Morison and Commager (*Growth of the American Republic*, 1, 244.) that the "in-

tellectual leader of the Republican party was Colonel John Taylor"—a statement nowhere supported in the rest of the book—is utterly without meaning. Taylor served in the Senate from 1792 to 1794, where according to Monroe, his colleague, he took almost no active part. Otherwise he was not on the national scene at all during the great period of the development of Republican policy. His books and pamphlets in defense of the Republican position normally appeared many years after controversies had died down. His attack on John Adams, for example, was finished more than twenty years after Adams's *Defence of the Constitutions of Government* appeared. It might well be added that Taylor's adherence to states'-rights was much more extreme, despite Jefferson's friendly endorsement, than the orthodox Republican position ever was.

3. The letter is given in Madison, *Writings*, II, 246-247, together with Madison's reply.

4. Madison, *Writings*, II, 246.

5. *Ibid.*, 247.

6. Madison, *Writings*, VI, 77.

7. *Annals of the Congress*, 8 April, 1789.

8. See Madison's letter to Hamilton, 19 November, 1789, in J. C. Hamilton, *History of the Republic*, IV, 60-64.

9. Madison, *Writings*, VI, 11.

10. The whole problem of the assumption is well discussed and fully documented in Brant's *Madison*, III, 306-318.

11. Madison, *Writings*, VI, 26.

12. *Ibid.*, 27.

13. *Ibid.*

14. *Ibid.*, 28-29.

15. Jefferson, "Opinion of the Secretary of State Against the Constitutionality of a National Bank," 15 February, 1791, *Writings*, V, 286.

16. *Ibid.*

17. Madison, *op. cit.*, 29.

18. *Ibid.*

19. *Ibid.*

20. *Ibid.*, 37.

21. *Ibid.*, 41.

22. Jefferson, *op. cit.*, 288-289. As late as 1816 Jefferson wrote to John Taylor of Caroline: "And I sincerely believe, with you, that banking establishments are more dangerous than standing armies; and that the principle of spending money to be paid by posterity, under the name of funding, is but swindling futurity on a large scale." (*Writings*, ed. Koch and Peden, 673.)

23. Madison, *Writings*, VI, 86, 23 January, 1792.

24. *Ibid.*, 104, 2 April, 1792.

25. *Ibid.*, 104-105.

26. *Ibid.*, 114-118, 26 September, 1792.

27. See Zoltan Haraszti, *John Adams and the Prophets of Progress*, 1952, 37 ff. for an excellent account of Adams's supposed "monarchism." It must be added, however, that to read either Madison or Adams, as Haraszti does, as deriving

their positions from "class struggle" is to read back into their views a notion which had no corresponding meaning in their time.

28. 13 August, 1791, *Writings*, ed. Ford, I, 168-169.
29. Feelings ran so high that principal leaders on both sides participated in the polemical warfare. Hamilton published under various pseudonyms a series of insidious attacks on Jefferson and Freneau. The long series appeared in Fenno's *Gazette of the United States* in 1792. A particularly effective series of answers, which first appeared in Dunlap's *American Daily Advertiser* and was reprinted by Fenno, has been shown by Philip March to have been the work of James Monroe, with assistance from Madison. See Marsh's *Monroe's Defense of Jefferson and Freneau Against Hamilton*, 1948.
30. Madison, *Writings*, VI, 98-99, 5 March, 1792.
31. *Ibid.*, 99.
32. *Ibid.*, 101, 29 March, 1792.
33. *Ibid.*, 102.
34. *Ibid.*, 103.
35. *Ibid.*, 221.
36. Washington, *Writings*, ed. Ford, XII, 491.
37. Madison, *Writings*, VI, 222.
38. Letter to Jefferson, 21 December, 1794, *Writings*, VI, 228-229.
39. Henry Adams, *Life of Albert Gallatin*, 1879, 115.
40. *Ibid.*, 117.
41. *Ibid.*, 172.
42. *Ibid.* 230,
43. *Ibid.*, 230-231.
44. *Ibid.*, 231.
45. *Ibid.*, 170.
46. Jefferson, *Writings*, VII, 327-329.
47. *The Jeffersonians*, 1951.
48. See his *Policy and Administration*, 1950.
49. See for example White, *The Jeffersonians*, 134-136.
50. *Writings*, ed. Ford, VIII, 2-3, First Inaugural, 4 March, 1801.
51. *Ibid.*, 3.
52. *Ibid.*, 119, Gallatin's notes and calculations are given here, pp. 109-117.
53. *Annals of Congress*, December 1794–January 1795. The whole question is discussed in Brant's *Madison* III, 420ff.
54. Jefferson, *ibid.*, 124.
55. *The New Yorker*, 3 January, 1953.
56. *Writings*, op. cit., 343-344.
57. White, in *The Jeffersonians*, gives the best available account of the whole matter, and I follow him closely.

Republics should approach near to each other. In many respects they all have the same interest.
— James Monroe, *Address to the French National Convention,* 1794.

CHAPTER FOUR
Foreign Policy

THE PROBLEM of the young American republic in adjusting her relations with other nations was of a magnitude almost unprecedented in the long history of the emergence of nation states. The independence secured in the war with Britain would remain nominal only, until the United States could conduct her commerce on a level of equality with other countries, secure her western and southern boundaries, and establish her credit in the markets of the world. Since so much of her strength and available resources had been expended in the war, she must move toward the realization of these objectives without again involving herself in a military struggle. Meanwhile, as an experiment in freedom, she labored under the additional handicap of posing a continuing threat to the internal security of the monarchies of Europe.

The scope of the problem and the limiting conditions within which it must be solved were appreciated by Federalists and Republicans alike. The objectives of peace and prosperous commerce were not matters of dispute. But below the level of grand abstraction the room for disagreement was boundless. In foreign policy means are seldom clearly distinguishable from ends, and foreign policy itself normally remains implicated with domestic policy. Thus a difference over the handling of the debt would lead almost immediately to a difference over commercial policy, and that difference, in turn, would lead to a difference over means best calculated to achieve peace. Similarly, a difference as to the sort of government best suited to the United States would lead to a difference as to the sort of foreign allies to be cultivated. "Republics,"

89

Monroe, as minister to France, told the French National Convention, "should approach near to each other."[1] But the Federalists countered with the cogent proposition that American commerce could hardly expect to flourish without the friendship of Britain, the dominant power on the seas. Since Britain and France were at war, the Americans could not have it both ways.

Most plain citizens in the United States, during the 1790's, as well as a good many members of Congress, regarded our foreign relations with an uncertainty mixed with substantial measures of ignorance and confusion. The long delays in communication and the lack of authentic information tended to perpetuate the latter two ingredients. But the leadership of the two parties was firm. And it is not necessary to make a detailed survey of American foreign relations in order to understand and assess the Republican position. Whether they took the lead in proposing measures, or attacked from any quarter, and however they negotiated or compromised on particular questions, the Republicans were guided by principles which followed coherently from their general view of the nature of government and their conception of the American Republic.

In one of his articles of 1792 in the *National Gazette*, Madison addressed himself to the theory of peace and laid down the fundamental position of the Republicans. He begins with a critical review of Rousseau's proposal for a league of sovereign powers. This notion, Madison argued, was unacceptable on two grounds: it would not remove the ambitions of monarchs, which were among the chief causes of wars; and it would tend to perpetuate the oppression of the people under monarchical subjugation. Rousseau, in any case, was a visionary. "A universal and perpetual peace, it is to be feared, is in the catalogue of events, which will never exist but in the imaginations of visionary philosophers, or in the breasts of benevolent enthusiasts."[2] But the folly and misery of war are so great that there must be no end to the effort to stop it. Proceeding as realistically as possible, Madison points out two chief classes of wars: those which follow from the will of governments without reference to the interests of the people; and those which accord with "the will of society itself."

The only means of preventing wars of the first sort is to bring the will of the people and the will of the government into harmony. "Whilst war is to be declared by those who are to spend the public money, not by those who are to pay it; by those who are to direct the public forces, not by those who are to support them; by those whose power is to be raised, not by those whose chains may be riveted, the disease must continue to be *hereditary* like the government of which it is the offspring." The only remedy is to "regenerate" the government—to make a democratic revolution and set up the representative forms of a republic. The United States had set an example by placing the power to declare war in the hands of Congress, to guarantee that any war of the United States should have popular support. This principle, and its constitutional implementation, provided the base, as we shall see, for the Republican attack on Washington's neutrality declaration of 1793.

Madison readily admits that the prevention of wars of the second class—those which do in fact have popular support—is a much more difficult problem. But "there are antidotes, nevertheless, which may not be without their efficacy." Thus:

> As wars of the first class were to be prevented by subjecting the will of the government to the will of society, those of the second class can only be controlled by subjecting the will of the society to the reason of the society; by establishing permanent and constitutional maxims of conduct, which may prevail over occasional impressions and inconsiderate pursuits.[3]

Madison offered two such maxims. It should, in the first place, be a matter of policy that any war must be paid for by the generation which enters into it. ("The earth belongs to the living.") It is not simply that one generation has not the right to bind another in law or debt, but that the burden of payment will prove the strongest kind of deterrent to aggressive action. To make sure that this is so, Madison adds his second maxim, that certain of the taxes needed to pay for a war should be levied so directly upon individuals that they are immediately aware of the impact. While it may be necessary to raise the larger portion of the necessary sums by the customary levies which are partly hidden, a significant share can still be raised directly—"a due proportion of such as by their direct operation keep the people awake, along with those, which being wrapped up in other payments, may leave them asleep, to misapplications of their money."[4] Thus "a public debt is a public curse" not only because it ties up the income of the people and frustrates their desire to improve their living standards, but because it facilitates a policy of aggression. As for wars of defense, Madison thought that no war could be imagined the expense of which could not be discharged within the lifetime of the generation participating in it. If, to the tax-hardened and debt-ridden citizen of the twentieth century, such a view seems fully as visionary as Rousseau's scheme seemed to Madison, the Repub-

lican philosopher might reply quickly enough that he never claimed his
maxims would be carried out—only that they might work if put into
practice.

The chief objection to Madison's maxims—an objection upon which
the Hamiltonian view was based—was that certain wars would so re-
dound to the benefit of future generations that it was entirely proper
for them to share the cost. Madison attacks this contention by pointing
out that in the nature of things there would be only one party to make
the decision in a two-way transaction, which is no proper or valid contract. Furthermore, the proposition rests on bad logic—"in the alternative of sacrificing exceptions to general rules, or of converting exceptions to general rules, the former is the lesser evil."[5] Madison might have
been reminded that he had himself, in debating with Jefferson the thesis
that the earth belongs always to the living generation, argued that certain expenditures binding the future to a debt might be justified by the
benefits they conferred upon the future. But the case was different as
regarded war. While the improvement of a harbor would certainly be
useful for an indefinite period, the decision to make war would involve
society in actions of which no man could foretell the outcome. In any
case the fruits of war are normally rotten. The point was to reap the
healthful harvest of peace.

> Were a nation to impose such restraints on itself, avarice would be
> sure to calculate the expenses of ambition; in the equipoise of these
> passions, reason would be free to decide for the public good; and an
> ample reward would accrue to the state, first, from the avoidance of
> all its wars of folly, secondly, from the vigor of its unwasted resour-
> ces for wars of necessity and defense. Were all nations to follow the
> example, the reward would be doubled to each; and the temple of
> Janus might be shut, never to be opened more.[6]

Such a position involved, above all, a counsel of patience. This was,
in fact, a virtue which, whatever else may be said of their foreign policy,
the Republicans did not lack. Fifteen years later John Quincy Adams
left the Federalist ranks to join the Republicans precisely because the
patience of President Jefferson, and of Madison as Secretary of State, in
the face of British provocation, had preserved peace and prosperity to a
point where the war that was to come would be widely popular and the
moral onus laid on the shoulders of the enemy. During the 1790's this
counsel of patience, together with their libertarian principles, led the
Republicans to condone the aggressive tactics of the French revolutionary governments to a point nearly beyond their own endurance, and
well beyond what seemed to Federalists the last outpost of patriotism.

In brief, Madison's theory of peace calls for the spread of republicanism throughout the world. There can be no safety for the common man until he controls his own government, and beyond that he must discipline himself to spend no more than what he earns. Domestic liberty and progress and international peace are, as with the Union, one and inseparable.

Thus Republican foreign policy began at home, with the effort to hold the powers of war and peace in the hands of the Congress as the elected representatives of the people, and to prevent the growth of a permanent debt. Beyond their own shores, the Republicans would cultivate a favorable bias toward republican countries and look with favor upon revolutions against any form of tyranny or irresponsible monarchic control. But since they must live in a world composed chiefly of monarchical states, they would rely, in peacetime relations, upon the principle of "free commerce with all nations; political connection with none," as Jefferson put it to Elbridge Gerry.

The Republican position respecting treaties and commerical agreements was established by Jefferson in his *Opinion on the Question whether the United States have a Right to renounce their Treaties with France* . . . , written at Washington's request in April, 1793. Jefferson developed his view by transferring the principles of the social contract as between members of one society to the relations between two societies, thus providing the "law of nations" with the same sanction as the civil governments of individual states:

> I consider the people who constitute a society or nation as the source of all authority in that nation; as free to transact their common concerns by any agents they think proper; to change these agents individually, or the organization of them in form or function whenever they please; that all the acts done by these agents under the authority of the nation, are the acts of the nation, are obligatory to them and enure to their use, and can in no wise be annulled or affected by any change in the form of the government, or of the persons administering it. . . .[7]

He discriminated three aspects of the law of nations: "1) The moral law of our nature. 2) The usages of nations. 3) Their special conventions." In considering the sanctity of treaties and commercial agreements, the first only was applicable:

> The moral duties which exist between individual and individual in a state of nature, accompany them into a state of society, and the aggregate of the duties of all the individuals composing the society constitutes the duties of that society towards any other; so that be-

tween society and society the same moral duties exist as did between
the individuals composing them, while in an unassociated state, and
their maker not having released them from those duties on their forming themselves into a nation.

Thus it follows that contracts drawn between nations have the same
sanction as the obligations of individuals to one another. It is worth noticing again, as we have done earlier, that Jefferson's notion of the "aggregate of the duties of all the individuals composing the society" pre-
cludes any organic or idealist theory of the state. It is because the agents
of a nation act in behalf of their constituents that the nation is obliged
by their acts. A nation is not an entity independent of its individual
citizens and has neither life nor function of its own, beyond the lives of
its citizens and the functions performed by their agents.

However, there are circumstances in which treaties do become in-
valid. Two criteria may be established. If the performance of an obligation becomes *impossible*, the obligation ceases to operate, both as
between individuals and as between nations. And if the performance of
an obligation would be *self-destructive* to one party, the obligation is
again invalidated by that fact. But these are extreme conditions, and it
does not follow that treaties or agreements may be suspended or voided
simply because they are "dangerous, useless, or disagreeable." Such
agreements are to be avoided in the first instance by wise consideration
of the national interest. If, by the force of unforeseen events, agreements do take on such unfavorable characters, they may be repudiated
only by the joint action of the contracting parties.

It is characteristic of Jefferson, as of his Republican colleagues, that
he appealed to reason for the support of these views. "For the reality of
these principles I appeal to the true fountains of evidence, the head and
heart of every rational and honest man. It is there nature has written her
moral laws, and where every man may read them for himself."[8] The
twentieth-century student of international relations and international
law may indeed be sceptical of such premises, but Jefferson would be
entitled to argue that no more reliable sanction has been discovered in
the intervening years.

To the principles of peace through the spreading of republican liberty, and the contractual obligation of international agreements, the Republicans added a third postulate to complete the theoretical structure
of their foreign policy—free trade. As we have seen, Madison laid
down this principle at the very beginning of business in the Congress

under the Constitution. "I own myself the friend to a very free system of commerce," he said, "and hold it as a truth that commercial shackles are generally unjust, oppressive and impolitic." In an age when mercantilist theories prevailed not only among the foreign ministries of the old world but among the Hamiltonians at home, the Republicans looked forward to expansion and prosperity through freedom of the seas and freedom of ships and cargoes. Some of them had read Adam Smith's *Wealth of Nations*, which appeared in 1776, and were clearly influenced by it. But had there been no *Wealth of Nations* there is no doubt that men like Jefferson, Madison, John Taylor, and Gallatin would have favored free trade as at once serving the interests of the United States and following logically and morally from republican definitions of individual liberty and right.[9] It would be an exaggeration to say that the Republicans had an articulated conception of "one world," but their adherence to isolation as a policy was confined to political matters, and their understanding of the inter-dependence of nations through the world market was genuinely prophetic.

II

The party battle over foreign policy, which nearly tore the American Republic apart in the 1790's, was owing more largely to the impact of the French Revolution than to any other circumstance. At the outset of the French upheaval, while Jefferson was still in Paris, the American reaction was favorable, even enthusiastic. The services of Lafayette, one of the chief French leaders, to the cause of the American Revolution, and the crucial aid of French soldiers and the French navy, were fresh in American memories. They could only welcome the overthrow of feudal tyranny by their great European ally. "Bliss was it in that dawn to be alive," wrote Wordsworth, "But to be young was very heaven." Editorial comment in the press expressed the feelings of the American people, and French emissaries received many assurances of good will and support from the government, including not only President Washington, but Hamilton and other Federalists. But as the ancient animosities between France and England became inflamed by the aggressive assertion of French revolutionary strength, American opinion began to find itself divided.

While the treaty with France had important advantages and the French proclamation of liberty answered to the libertarian ideals of the

Americans, it was also important to develop favorable relations with Britain. The British had not honored the treaty of 1783. The western posts were still occupied by British troops, the Mississippi was not effectually open to commerce, and American shipping was under constant hazard on the high seas. The United States was too weak to oppose the British navy and felt herself too dependent on British markets to warrant a serious rupture.

Nor would the temper of the times allow a dispassionate calculation of American interest. Emotions were aroused and party friction exacerbated by the appearance, in 1791, of Burke's *Reflections on the Revolution in France* and Tom Paine's *The Rights of Man*. Burke's assertion of the ethical and political values of order and tradition, and his drawing of the classic distinction between liberty and license, appealed to the Federalists as not only an unanswerable attack on the French Revolution but a cogent defense of their own domestic program. Paine, on the other hand, proclaiming once more the inalienable rights of man and the liberty of the individual against the state, seemed to the Republicans to bring new life to the spirit of the American Revolution and to bind it to the French with ideal ties. When a Philadelphia bookseller prefaced his edition of Paine's pamphlet with a letter of praise by Jefferson (not intended for publication) the party line was clearly drawn, and thereafter very few were rash enough to cross it. It might be said that the tragic play was now on the boards, and such struggles as those over the debt and the bank seemed like mere curtain-raisers.

By the spring of 1793 the tension had increased, as Britain and France went to war, to a point where Washington was forced to take direct action. Hamilton, in the Cabinet, argued that the French treaty of 1778 should be suspended or nullified. He based his contention on the principle that the treaty which had been negotiated with the French monarchy, was no longer binding, since the French had altered their form of government by the establishment of a republic. Jefferson replied, in his written opinion, that the treaty was "not between the United States and Louis Capet, but between the two nations of America and France; and the nations remaining in existence, though both of them have since changed their forms of government," the treaty was not annulled by such changes.[10] He proceeded to apply his theory of the sanctity of international agreements under all circumstances save "impossibility" or "self-destruction," and asserted that in this case the obligations could be claimed, at worst, merely to be "dangerous, useless or disagreeable." Moving from the theory into concrete considerations, he then undertook to show that in fact the obligations were none of these things. They were not dangerous, since France had made no demand that the United States join in the war, as she could if her western islands were attacked; they were not useless, since they brought a fruitful commerce; and they were not disagreeable, since they bound us to the support of liberty.

Hamilton had appealed to the law of nations to support his case, citing the Swiss jurist Vattel: "for it [a nation] may say with truth, that it would not have allied itself with this nation, if it had been under the present form of its government." Jefferson, for his part, appealed to two older authorities, Grotius and Pufendorf, as well as other passages from Vattel, to discount this view. But as a Republican he could not be content with a merely scholarly victory. He forced his point home with deadly political effect. The conclusion of Vattel's sentence, he said, "suggests a reflection too strong to be suppressed". . . .

The republic of the United States allied itself with France when under a despotic government. She changes her government, and declares it shall be a republic; prepares a form of republic extremely free, and in the meantime is governing herself as such. And it is proposed that America shall declare the treaties void, because it may say with truth that it would not have allied itself with that nation if it had been under the present form of its government. Who is the American who can say with truth that he would not have allied himself to France if she had been a republic? Or that a republic of any form would be as disagreeable as her ancient despotism?[11]

Washington, partly heeding Jefferson's advice—and for the last time—decided to compromise. He proclaimed the *neutrality* of the United States in relation to the European war. This action conformed in certain respects with Republican wishes as to policy, as well as Federalist. But the Republicans objected strenuously to the method of an executive proclamation, and precipitated a fundamental debate on the extent of executive power to make foreign policy.

The proclamation was issued on April 22. Early in May, Madison wrote to Jefferson, "Peace is no doubt to be preserved at any price that honor and good faith will permit. But it is no less to be considered that the least departure from these will not only be most likely to end in the loss of peace, but is pregnant with every other evil that could happen to us."[12] A month later he wrote again, more forcefully:

The proclamation was in truth a most unfortunate error. It wounds the national honor, by seeming to disregard the stipulated duties to

France. It wounds the popular feelings by a seeming indifference to the cause of liberty. And it seems to violate the forms and spirit of the Constitution, by making the executive Magistrate the organ of the disposition, the duty, and the interest of the nation in relation to war and peace, subjects appropriated to other departments of the government.[13]

Monroe, also writing to Jefferson, announced himself an advocate of peace "against every invitation to war." He would ignore, so far as humanly possible, the insults and irritations of Britain or Spain. He would wish to help France in any way short of war. But "to expose ourselves to their fury (i.e. the provocations of European nations) would be as imprudent" as for a man in health to expose himself to a lunatic. "To preserve peace will no doubt be difficult, but by accomplishing it, we show our wisdom and magnanimity. We secure to our people the enjoyment of a dignified repose, by indulging which they will be prosperous and happy."[14] On the other hand, he could not conceive upon what principle the right to issue the neutrality proclamation was claimed:

I think the position incontrovertible that if he [Washington] possesses the right to say we shall be neutral, he might say we should not be. The power in both instances must be in the same hands, for if the Executive could say we should be neutral, how could the Legislature, that we should war. In truth a right to declare our neutrality, as a distinct authority, cannot exist, for that is only the natural state of things, when the positive power of declaring war is not exerted; and this belongs to the Legislature only; any interference therefore with it, by the Executive, must be unconstitutional and improper.[15]

The Republican position was intrinsically difficult to maintain. They wished to support France. But they wished to remain neutral. By attacking the proclamation, they appeared to be for war on the side of France. What was still worse, it was precisely the time at which Genet, the new ambassador from France, was outraging American public opinion, including the Republicans, by his brash appeals to the people over the head of the government. Hamilton, under the pseudonym of "Pacificus," was defending the proclamation and denouncing the Republicans in a powerful series of papers in the *Gazette of the United States*. The Republican Party, in fact, was almost swamped when Jefferson wrote to Madison, on July 7th, "Nobody answers him [Hamilton] and his doctrines will therefore be taken for confessed. For God's sake, my dear sir, take up your pen, select the most striking heresies and cut him to pieces in the face of the public. There is nobody else who can and will enter the lists with him."[16] Madison, somewhat grudgingly, did so in a series of essays under the name of "Helvidius."

The key to the Helvidius papers, as representative of the Republican position, is that they dealt entirely with the questions of principle and constitutional authority. France was scarcely mentioned, though the opening sentence was strong enough—"Several pieces with the signature of *Pacificus* were lately published, which have been read with singular pleasure and applause, by the foreigners and degenerate citizens among us, who hate our republican government, and the French revolution; whilst the publication seems to have been too little regarded, or too much despised by the steady friends of both."[17]

The main force of the argument is contained in the first of the series of six papers. After a number of direct quotations to show that Hamilton rested his case on the claim that foreign relations are, in general, the affair of the executive, and that the powers to declare war and to ratify treaties and appointments of diplomatic officials are exceptions not controlling the principle, Madison summarizes the Federalist position as follows:

That the powers of declaring war and making treaties are, in their nature, executive powers. . . .

That being particularly vested by the constitution in other departments, they are to be considered as exceptions out of the general grant to the executive department. . . .

That the executive, consequently, as the organ of intercourse with foreign nations, and the interpreter and executor of treaties, and the law of nations, is authorized to expound all articles of treaties, those involving questions of war and peace, as well as others. . . .

That in particular the executive had power to judge, whether in the case of the mutual guarantee between the United States and France, the former were bound by it to engage in the war. . . .

The basis of the reasoning is, we perceive, the extraordinary doctrine, that the powers of making war, and treaties, are in their nature executive; and therefore comprehended in the general grant of executive power. . . .[18]

He then proceeds to examine whether these doctrines can be supported by the writings of authorities on law or by the Constitution.

Madison cites writers like Wolsius, Burlemaqui, and Vattel as holding that the powers to make treaties and declare war are among the "highest acts of the sovereignty," which must necessarily include the legislative branch under a constitutional government. While both Locke and

Montesquieu appear to vest these powers in the executive, Madison points out that Locke saw them as "really distinct" from regular executive functions. The difficulty with all of these authorities, he argues, is that they are writing about monarchies, so that their judgments are largely irrelevant to the problems of a republic. In a footnote he observes, "The chapter [of Locke] on prerogative shows, how much the reason of the philosopher was clouded by the royalism of the Englishman." In a letter to Jefferson, covering the manuscript of this essay, Madison told his friend to eliminate the passages dealing with writers on law if they seemed to be ineffective, "my doubts as to that proceed from the danger of turning the controversy too much in the wilderness of books."[19] Jefferson left them as they stood, but Madison passed on quickly, "let us quit a field of research which is more likely to perplex than to decide."

The heart of the argument lies in the application of the principle of the separation of powers, whose purpose is to protect the liberties of the people and secure their control over their government. The two following passages are of central importance:

> The natural province of the executive magistrate is to execute laws, as that of the legislature is to make laws. All his acts, therefore, properly executive, must presuppose the existence of the laws to be executed. A treaty is not an execution of laws; it does not presuppose the existence of laws. It is, on the contrary, to have itself the force of a *law*, and to be carried into *execution*, like all *other laws*, by the *executive magistrate*. To say then that the power of making treaties, which are confessedly laws, belongs naturally to the department which is to execute laws, is to say, that the executive department naturally includes a legislative power. In theory this is an absurdity—in practice a tyranny.

Madison, of course, states the case severely, for polemical reasons. He knew well enough that such distinctions can never be absolute. But the compelling force of the argument served the Republicans to advantage for many years. It formed the basis, as we shall see, of their attack on the Jay Treaty and other Federalist measures. And again it may be observed that they were singularly consistent. While Jefferson initiated the purchase of Louisiana in contradiction to Madison's doctrine (and his own), he faced the fact and asked for a constitutional amendment to cover such actions. In later years many similar cases have occurred, but the principle has never been discarded. Lincoln's emancipation of the slaves in 1863 was generally regarded as without the force of law until the Thirteenth Amendment was enacted. And as recently as the spring of 1952 the Supreme Court invalidated President Truman's seizure of the steel industry on the ground that the executive has no inherent powers of the sort that Madison called legislative. It is worth noting, in addition, that the quasi-legislative powers of the modern executive, so much under discussion in recent years, derive not from constitutional interpretation but from the necessity of rule making under circumstances in which Congress has enacted very broad and general statutes.

Madison now proceeds directly to the question of war and peace:

A declaration that there shall be war, is not an execution of laws: it does not suppose pre-existing laws to be executed: it is not, in any respect, an act merely executive. It is, on the contrary, one of the most deliberate acts that can be performed; and when performed, has the effect of *repealing* all the *laws* operating in a state of peace, so far as they are inconsistent with a state of war; and of *enacting*, as a *rule for the executive, a new* code adapted to the relation between the society and its foreign enemy. In like manner, a conclusion of peace *annuls* all the *laws* peculiar to a state of war, and *revives* the general *laws* incident to a state of peace.[20]

It follows from these considerations that, while the executive is properly charged with conducting foreign relations, according to law, and with negotiating treaties or advising on peace or war, it has no authority to be "that essential agency which gives validity to such determinations." Yet this was precisely what Washington had done, in the Republican view. Madison had already, in his essay on peace, indicated the dangers inherent in such action. Here was an example of precisely that irresponsible executive behavior which republican revolutions were intended to prevent, and which, as Madison attempted to show, was one of the most common causes of war. The line of demarcation might at times be indistinct, but he proposed to hold it in any case. It was not simply that Washington's proclamation did violence to a treaty, nor that France was deserving of republican sympathy—it was a question of the kind of government which was to prevail in the United States.

With debatable exceptions, Madison's doctrine has always guided the formal attitude of the American executive toward war and peace. The Korean War is a fair example. While some members of President Truman's opposition claimed that he had exceeded his authority in ordering American troops into Korea in the summer of 1950, that he should have asked Congress for a declaration of war, the legal point was clear enough. It may be that in common parlance it is confusing, or even rhetorical, to refer to an engagement which involves many thousands of casualties as a "police action." But the fact is, nevertheless, that in law the commitment of American troops was in the character of police against aggression as defined by the United Nations. The relation of the United States to the United Nations is governed by treaty, ratified by the Senate in accordance with the provisions of the Constitution, and concurred in by the House of Representatives through the appropriation of money to execute the treaty. As we shall see, shortly, Madison attempted to nullify the Jay Treaty by withholding funds for its execution, but once the appropriations had been voted he recognized the treaty as having the force of law and binding on all citizens.

In the latter portion of this first Helvidius paper, Madison measures Hamilton's doctrine of the supremacy of the executive against the Constitution. The analysis is similar in method to his handling of the question of the national bank. He cites the clauses which might be claimed as authority and shows, one by one, that they will not suffice, or that to employ them is to distort their plain meaning, or that they flatly contradict the claim. When all the specific powers of the President have been dismissed in this fashion, there remain only the joint powers of the President and the Senate to make treaties. But these have already been shown to give no sanction to Washington's proclamation. And so, Madison asks, where might Hamilton have borrowed his opinions? "There is but one answer to this question. The power of making treaties and the power of declaring war, are *royal prerogatives* in the British government, and are accordingly treated as executive *prerogatives* by *British commentators.*"[21] Thus the political tables are turned. The proclamation favors the British, and the arguments in defense of it depend upon the theory and practice of the British government. What is worse, "Pacificus," once upon a time "when no application to *persons or measures* could bias," had taken a quite different view. In the *Federalist* Hamilton had written, "though several writers on the subject of government place that power [of making treaties] in the class of *executive authorities,* yet this is *evidently* an *arbitrary disposition.* For if we attend *carefully* to its operation, it will be found to partake *more* of the *legislative* than of the *executive* character. . . ."[22]

Whether in this, and the subsequent papers which elaborated on these themes, Madison cut Hamilton to pieces, as Jefferson demanded, may be debated. But the clarity of the argument and the cogency and force with which Washington's right to issue a proclamation of neutrality was attacked, provided the Republicans with an indispensable ingredient in their developing foreign policy. Like his colleague Gallatin in domestic policy, Madison showed that the most effective opposition would be at once critical and creative.

III

The principal development of Republican commercial policy arose in a series of positive studies and proposals not involving a direct attack on the administration. Among his final duties as Secretary of State, Jefferson prepared for the House a report on the international trade of the United States, with particular attention to duties and restrictions charged against American commerce and navigation. In addition to presenting a detailed set of balance sheets, he took the occasion to develop a theory of free trade and reciprocal tariffs. Urging upon the Congress a policy of entering into bi-lateral reciprocal agreements, Jefferson thus expressed his view:

Instead of embarrassing commerce under piles of regulating laws, duties and prohibitions, could it be relieved from all its shackles in all parts of the world, could every country be employed in producing that which nature has best fitted it to produce, and each be free to exchange with others mutual surpluses for mutual wants, the greatest mass possible would be produced of those things which contribute to human life and human happiness; the numbers of mankind would be increased, and their condition bettered.[23]

Recognizing the practical impossibility of instituting such a policy among all nations, or even among many, he urged that it nevertheless be commenced even if only with one nation. As conditions altered, one country after another might be added to the system until all should, ideally, be included. In bi-lateral agreements certain items might be excepted in accordance with the particular needs or expedients of either nation. In such cases freedom should be modified only with reference to these particulars and by "mutual and equivalent measures, preserving it entire in all others." Other nations, not yet prepared for free trade, might be approached in terms of proposals of "reciprocating the duties to be levied on each side, or in compensating any excess of duty by equivalent advantages of another nature."

The assumption underlying Jefferson's position was that the United States would remain and develop as primarily a producer of food and raw materials and a consumer of the manufactures of the old world. Domestic manufacture should be encouraged only to fill gaps in the economy or to supply wants where war or other international difficulties choked off normal channels. The system, Jefferson thought, would bring prosperity and steadily increasing population to an expanding United States, which would in turn provide so large a market as to keep the manufacturing nations of Europe in full employment.

But Jefferson's theory was no idle dream. He proposed to be firm enough with nations which were unwilling to co-operate. The United States had a profound obligation to protect its citizens and their commerce and navigation with strong counter-measures against prohibitions, duties, and regulations. "Free commerce and navigation are not to be given in exchange for restrictions and vexations; nor are they likely to produce a relaxation of them."[24] In practice, then, the United States should adopt a scheme of discriminating duties, based on the principle of one set of moderate charges for those who favor our produce, another set of much higher charges for those who do not, and a parallel policy designed to give as much support as possible to American ships and seamen by reciprocal agreements or penalties depending on the attitudes of other nations.

In the House, on January 4th, 1794, Madison offered a series of resolutions which would guide the Congress in translating Jefferson's proposals into law. The resolutions followed the *Report* closely, but went further in terms of protection for American merchants. Madison insisted that it was the obligation of government to exact damages from foreign governments guilty of depredations on American commerce, or, failing that, to make restitution from the treasury of the United States. His final resolution called for reimbursing losses, incurred through foreign regulations in violation of the law of nations, "out of the additional duties on the manufactures, productions, and vessels of the nation establishing such unlawful regulations."[25]

The Republican policy, thus worked out by Jefferson and Madison, ran sharply contrary to the philosophy of Hamilton's *Report on Manufactures* and was strongly opposed by him. But even though the most immediate effect of the program would occur in the risk of a more seriously aggravated trade war with Britain, the greater number of Federalist leaders were so deeply involved in shipping, rather than manufacture, that it had fair prospects of enactment. A test vote in the House showed that it had firm support. But it was almost immediately shelved in the face of still more outrageous abuses of American commerce by the British in the West Indies. A temporary embargo was agreed upon, and the administration prepared to send a special mission to London.

In the terms proposed by Madison the Republican program was never fully realized, because of the continuing struggle with Britain. In another generation the drive for manufacture brought the industrial revolution to the United States, as Hamilton had hoped. For more than a hundred years the question of protective tariffs as against free trade characterized the American party division. The issue became bitterly sectional and tended to lose its principled basis. But from the vantage point of the mid-twentieth century it is difficult to deny that the Republican policy of the 1790's was well grounded in the enduring needs of mankind. The old Republicans would have applauded the reciprocal trade policy of Cordell Hull in the administrations of Franklin Roosevelt, and cheered enthusiastically the call of men like Henry Ford II for an end to all tariff barriers. Should the World Trade Organization and other agencies of the United Nations one day find it possible to carry out their program, the Republican dream would indeed be actualized.

IV

The administration view of the needs and position of the United States in 1794 is amply indicated by Washington's original thought of sending Hamilton to negotiate with the British. The Secretary of the Treasury was the strongest American friend of the British and their form of government, and had for several years moved behind the scenes to undermine the efforts of Jefferson, as Secretary of State, to make friendly overtures to France and to support the French Revolution. Jefferson had, for his part, frequently attempted to interfere in the affairs of the Treasury. The Party issue was so bitter that Hamilton's appointment could not have been confirmed. Monroe, writing to Jefferson with acid humor, thought it "more suitable to employ John Dickinson, who I believe drew the last petition of Congress to the king, in the course of the late revolution."[26] A few days later he undertook, as a senator, to give Washington gratuitous advice against the appointment of Hamilton:

Sir, Having casually heard that it was requested by many of Colo. Hamilton's political associates, that you would nominate him as Envoy to the Court of Great Britain, and as I should deem such a measure not only injurious to the public interest, but also especially so to your own, I have taken the liberty to express that sentiment to you and likewise to observe farther, that in case it is your wish I should explain to you more at large my reason for this opinion, I will wait on you at any hour you may appoint for that purpose. . . .[27]

Though Washington's reply was coldly formal, Hamilton's name was never sent to the Senate, and Chief Justice John Jay, an experienced diplomat, was chosen instead. But Jay was a Federalist, and Monroe voted against confirmation. Jefferson, Madison, and the other Republicans shared with Monroe the belief that Jay was a vain man, pro-British, and certain to be outwitted in the diplomatic game.

The administration felt the force of the opposition keenly, and fearing also that the French would react unfavorably to Jay's mission, decided to send a Republican as minister to France, succeeding the Federalist Gouverneur Morris whose recall had been requested by the French government. After political soundings had been taken and considerable negotiation, Monroe himself was nominated and accepted the appointment. This appointment, incredible by modern standards, can only be understood in terms of the fact that intense party spirit had not yet produced the party system. Though the Federalists had the dominant voice, Washington was still attempting to carry out his policy of receiving both parties into his administration and making them work together. Without questioning the President's motives (at the outset), the Republicans were less ingenuous. Anticipating only the worst from Jay's mission, they seized upon the opportunity for Monroe to go to Paris as a fortunate accident which might enable them to save Franco-American relations from complete ruin, and so to preserve the republican orientation of the United States. Thus occurred the tragic paradox of two parallel American missions, charged with preserving the safety of the country, headed by leading figures of bitterly opposing parties, who held each other personally in contempt as to both character and policy. The result was foredoomed: Jay's mission resulting in the most controversial American agreement before Yalta, and Monroe's in his dramatic recall for "misconduct." Historians have ranged in their evaluation of Jay's treaty from the view that it was the best obtainable and a proper means of avoiding war, to Henry Adams's judgment that at no time after 1800 (when the Republicans came to power) would the United States have accepted terms so humiliating. Some historians have seen Monroe as a hero of republican democracy, while others, like Morison and Commager, think that he "lost his balance and his usefulness." But our concern is only with the Republican side of the episode, as it illuminates Republican theory and practice in foreign affairs.

Monroe was guided throughout his three years in France by those principles of his party which we have already considered: he believed that the cause of peace and humanity required close fraternal relations between republics; that treaties of alliance were sacred obligations; and that the best commerce was free commerce. While, as an American minister, he was obliged to secure so far as he could the self-interest of his country, he saw no inconsistency between the purposes of his mission and his general principles. He was armed with documents which seemed to him more than adequate evidence that there was no misunderstanding between himself and the administration. Before his departure both Houses of Congress passed formal resolutions expressing renewed friendship for the French Revolution and once again acknowledging the old debts of gratitude to the French nation. The President, through a letter of transmittal by Secretary of State Edmund Randolph, himself an in-and-out Republican, added his assurances to the resolutions. Monroe's detailed instructions reiterated this theme, and offered sufficient latitude for warm and friendly overtures.

Randolph's instructions, to which Monroe ever after appealed in defense of his conduct, provide a clear insight into the American dilemma. The document begins with an explanation of "the real sentiments of the Executive, relative to the French nation."[28] Washington is represented as an early and continuing friend of the French Revolution, who wishes only for its success and freedom from outside interference. On the other hand, since French affairs have been undergoing many fluctuations, Monroe is to take care lest he attach himself to any particular party save as it appears "to go with the sense of the nation." He is to assume that the American policy of neutrality involves no intention on the part of the United States to withdraw from treaty obligations, but, on the contrary, that this policy best suits the interests of the French and is desired by them.

In the most crucial instruction, Randolph authorizes Monroe to say that the United States means to follow that same line of friendly and valuable conduct in the future. He is expressly told to "remove all jealousy with respect to Mr. Jay's mission to London," and to say that Jay "is positively forbidden to weaken the engagements between this country and France." This, for Monroe, was the heart of the matter:

It is not improbable, that you will be obliged to encounter, on this head, suspicions of various kinds. But you may declare the motives of that mission to be, to obtain immediate compensation for our plundered property, and restitution of the posts.

Monroe was then told that he might "intimate, but without ascribing it to the government," that if necessary the United States would go to war on the side of France, and that such action would be facilitated if the people were persuaded that every effort had been made to prevent it. Further, "you will be amply justified in repelling with firmness any imputation of the most distant intention to sacrifice our connection with France to any connection with England." Since the United States is a free republic, European refugees will seek asylum there, but even though many such persons should be Frenchmen fleeing from the Revolution, Monroe must see to it that this fact is not interpreted as any "estrangement from the French cause."

In a passage as quaint as it is revealing, Randolph strictly warns Monroe to counteract the stories he will hear that the United States is torn by a struggle of political parties. "If this intelligence should be used, in order to inspire a distrust of our good will to France, you will industriously obviate such an effect."

In later paragraphs Randolph directed Monroe to seek compensation for depredations on American commerce; to look after the interests of individual Americans having claims against France; to review American personnel serving in France to make sure that all were acceptable to the French government; to defend the embargo as meaning no slight to France; to undertake no negotiations of commercial or other alliances, but to refer such matters, should they arise, back to Philadelphia; and, finally, to move as far as he could to secure French help in freeing the Mississippi to American commerce. There is even a hint that, for this latter purpose, he might lend assistance should Spain wish a separate peace with France. The document concludes with further assurances of American good will to France. *"You will let it be seen, that in case of war, with any nation on earth, we shall consider France as our first and natural ally."* Randolph himself put this sentence into italics, as he did the clauses on Jay's mission.

This remarkable state paper is dated June 9, a time at which Jay was already in London, negotiating with the British not only on matters of compensation and securing the western posts, but on the whole range of commercial business and the definition of rights on the seas. What is chiefly remarkable about this juxtaposition is not so much the evident duplicity of administration policy, which was a simple reflection of the American dilemma, as the apparent tendency to suppose that it would succeed. If there is any justification for the vulgar tradition that Americans are sluggish and naive in the handling of their relations with Europe, there would seem to be a precedent in these early efforts at playing one great nation against another.

In any case it is clear that Monroe never had a chance of success, and easy enough to see why he soon concluded that he was the dupe of a partisan maneuver. A government dominated by Federalists with a pro-British slant could scarcely be expected to support a Republican who was pro-French. But Monroe made the best of his opportunity to advance the Republican position, and even his recall and "disgrace" were quickly turned into political capital.

Monroe showed his colors immediately upon his arrival in Paris. He waited a few days for an invitation to appear before the Committee of Public Safety and present his credentials. But when this was not forthcoming he wrote directly to the National Convention, which not only recognized him but invited him to appear and make a public address before it. His brief speech has no parallel in the history of American diplomacy. After acknowledging the honor done him by allowing him to address the French nation ("for all the citizens of France are represented here"), Monroe developed the theme of republican fraternity:

Republics should approach near to each other. In many respects they all have the same interest. But this is more especially the case with the American and French Republics:—their governments are similar; they both cherish the same principles and rest on the same basis, the equal and unalienable rights of men. The recollection too of common dangers and difficulties will increase their harmony, and cement their union. America had her day of oppression, difficulty and war, but her sons were virtuous and brave and the storm passed and left them in the enjoyment of peace, liberty and independence. France our ally and our friend and who aided in the contest, has now embarked in the same noble career; and I am happy to add that whilst the fortitude, magnanimity and heroic valor of her troops, command the admiration and applause of the astonished world, the wisdom and firmness of her councils unite equally in securing the happiest result.

He then adduced the resolutions of Congress and the President's message to support what he had said and to show that the people of America spoke with his voice. He concluded with an expression of his personal hope:

> that by doing everything in my power to preserve and perpetuate the harmony so happily subsisting at present between the two Republics, I shall promote the interest of both. To this great object therefore all my efforts will be directed. If I shall be so fortunate as to succeed in such manner as to merit the approbation of both Republics I shall deem it the happiest event of my life, and return hereafter with a consolation, which those who mean well and have served the cause of liberty alone can feel.[29]

It was a touching performance—pastoral, perhaps, in its hope for a liberated and fraternal world; tragic also, as it violated every accepted canon of diplomatic behavior. The French were, of course, delighted as well as surprised. The British were annoyed. The government in Philadelphia was astounded and dismayed. Monroe was immediately warned that he had exceeded the bounds of his instructions and must henceforward observe the greatest caution. But he was not repudiated. Whether his reprimand was justified depends, of course, on the justification for all normal diplomacy. Yet within the limits of the documents provided him, as distinct from the general usages of international relations, he could and did point to such a passage as this of Randolph, "That under the standard of liberty, wheresoever it shall be displayed, the affection of the United States will always rally: And that the successes of those who stand forth as her avengers will be gloried in by the United States, and will be felt as the successes of themselves and the other friends of humanity."[30] Monroe's great error, he was informed from home, was not that he had conveyed such sentiments to the French government, but that he had done so publicly. He made no apology. The resolutions of the Congress were a part of the public record, and he professed to see nothing wrong in making a speech about them. He knew well enough that there was an important distinction between handing documents to the chiefs of a foreign state in a private audience and delivering a public address of flattery which would irritate and disturb relations with other powers. But Monroe was concerned to make republican propaganda wherever he could, and his letters to his Republican friends make it clear that he acted deliberately.

Writing to Jefferson on September 7, he explains what he has done to open his relations with the French government, and adds, "Many incidents have since turned up to show the pleasure with which the organized departments and the people generally have received a mission from our republic to theirs, and I have every reason to believe that it will not only remove any previous existing solicitude, but tend to increase permanently the harmony between the two countries."³¹ The whole letter is redolent of optimism. Monroe tells his friend of the successes of French troops, of the harmonious atmosphere which has settled down since the fall of Robespierre and the end of the Terror (as he thought). There were abundant signs that the revolutionary spirit of liberty was spreading about Europe, as the coalition of kings gave way before the valor and might of French arms:

The spirit of liberty begins to show itself in other regions. Geneva has undergone revolution—the people have taken the government into their hands, apprehended the aristocrats, and executed seven of the most wicked. And in Poland under the direction of Kosciusko who acted with us in America, a formidable head has been raised against Prussia and Russia.

His enthusiasm even allowed him, for a moment, to expect success from Jay's mission to London. The severe pressure of France and her new allies against Britain, combined with renewed friendship between France and the United States would, he thought, induce the British to accept American demands and restore fruitful relations as well as the terms of the 1783 treaty. In another week his high hopes were symbolized by official notification from Geneva that the flags of the three republics had been hung side by side in the hall of the National Convention there. "The standards of republics should always be ranged together," he replied, "and I am perfectly satisfied, that this event will be received with equal joy by the government and citizens of the United States. . . ."³²

But by December news regarding the terms of Jay's treaty, which was signed in November, began to leak. From the moment of the first rumors Monroe's position deteriorated. It is not necessary to go over here the events of the next two years, as he tried at first to learn the terms of the treaty so that France might be forewarned and her displeasure forestalled, and then to convince the French government that the treaty, once published and ratified, did not really mean what it said. There is no doubt that Monroe did his best to protect the interest of the United States, and even achieved certain successes, chief of which was to delay until the end of 1796 a formal protest by the French that the Jay Treaty violated the Franco-American alliance. But there is no doubt, either, that he let his feelings be generally known, both to Republican friends at home and to French officials, in a manner clearly insubordinate by modern standards, though understandable in the context of his own peculiar situation. Jay, he thought, was no less than a traitor; the French had been cheated and their good will bartered for nothing; the Republicans had been malignantly duped; and he himself had been cruelly victimized. All this he wrote, in increasingly bitter letters, to Jefferson and Madison, including details of his actions and his relations with the French government which were not always reported to his superiors in Philadelphia.[33] Some of these letters found their way into the press. But, until the end of 1796, he continued to be useful to his government in delaying actions and in negotiating for the free navigation of the Mississippi. His loyalty, according to his own standards, was confirmed by his efforts to prevent Thomas Paine, whose release from French prison he had secured, from writing against Washington while a resident in the home of the American minister. But at length his behaviour became intolerable to the administration, and he was recalled and reprimanded for "misconduct."

Monroe's return to Philadelphia in June of 1797 brought the party battle to its highest point of tension thus far. To the Republicans he was a hero of liberty. Gallatin reported to his wife in a letter which well summarizes the Republican view of the whole episode:

Mr. Monroe arrived last night. . . . I spent two hours with him, during which he gave us (Jefferson and Burr, who is also in town) much interesting information, chiefly in relation to his conduct and to that of the Administration respecting himself and France. It appears that he was desirous, as soon as the treaty had been concluded by Jay, that it should be communicated to him, in order that he might lay it with candor and at once before the Committee of Public Safety; and he apprehends that if that mode had been adopted, France, under the then circumstances, would have been satisfied, would have accepted some verbal explanations, and would not have taken any further steps about it. But he never got the treaty until it appeared in the newspapers in August, 1795. . . . The French government received it, of course, indirectly and without any previous preparations having been made to soften them. Yet did Mr. Monroe, unsupported by the Administration here, without having any but irritating letters to show, for seven months stop their proceedings, giving thereby full time to our Administration to send powers or any conciliatory propositions which might promote an accommodation. But the precious time was lost, and worse than lost; and it is indeed doubtful whether for a certain length of time it will be possible to make *any* accommodation.

The time they chose to recall Monroe was when from his correspondence they had reason to believe that he had succeeded in allaying the resentment of the French. Then, thinking they had nothing to fear from France, and that they had used Monroe so as to obtain every service that he could render, they recalled him, with the double view of giving to another person the merit of terminating the differences and of throwing upon him (Monroe) the blame of any that had existed before. They were, however, deceived as to the fact, for, in spite of his honest endeavors, as soon as the final vote of the House of Representatives in favor of the treaty was known in France (and long before the letters of recall had reached that country) the die was cast. Upon the whole, I am happy to tell you that from my conversation with Monroe, from his manner and everything about him (things which are more easily felt than expressed), I have the strongest impression upon my mind that he is possessed of integrity superior to all the attacks of malignity, and that he had conducted himself with irreproachable honor and the most dignified sense of duty. Sorry I am to be obliged to add that I am also pretty well convinced that the American Administration have acted with a degree of meanness only exceeded by their folly, and that they have degraded the American name throughout Europe.[34]

A day or so later, the Republicans gave Monroe a "splendid dinner," attended by Jefferson (Vice-President of the United States!) and some fifty members of Congress. After a short but scorching correspondence with Timothy Pickering, the new Secretary of State who had fired him, Monroe went home to write a book in defense of his mission and of Republican policy. But before turning our attention to the book and the controversy it provoked, it is important to consider the implications of the attack which the Republicans had made on the Jay Treaty in the House of Representatives, where, as Gallatin said, the crucial vote was taken.

The treaty, which had been signed by Jay in November, 1794, was ratified by the Senate and signed by the President some six months later, and finally proclaimed, after British reconsideration, on February 29, 1796. The next day Washington sent the treaty to both Houses of Congress, since it required several legislative measures to bring about its implementation. This gave the Republicans their only real opportunity to oppose it. Edward Livingston opened the debate by offering a resolution calling upon the President to send to the House copies of Jay's instructions and other relevant papers. The Federalists immediately de-

nied the power of the House to call for such documents from the executive, on the ground that the treaty-making power was a sovereign
function of the President and the Senate.

Ostensibly the controversy turned upon the interpretation of conflicting provisions in the Constitution, where it is asserted, on the one
hand, that the Congress shall make all laws, and on the other, that treaties shall have the force of law. But the Republicans were concerned
with the more far-reaching implication of extending the executive
power by including within it a legislative function. As Gallatin put it,
"if the treaty-making power is not limited by existing laws, or if it re-
peals the laws that clash with it, or if the legislature is obliged to repeal
the laws so clashing, then the legislative power in fact resides in the
President and Senate, and they can, by employing an Indian tribe, pass
any law under the color of a treaty."[35] The argument was unanswerable,
and the Republicans won the first round when the House gave a substantial majority to Livingston's resolution.

Washington flatly refused to send the papers, denying the House any
right to concern itself with the treaty-making power. He exacerbated
the constitutional controversy by referring to his own presence at the
Constitutional Convention as witness to the intentions of the delegates.
This was an almost fatal blunder for the Federalist interest. The House
Republicans were, of course, led by Madison, who had been the leading
figure in the Convention and spoke with more authority than anyone
else on constitutional questions. In the course of a speech on April 6th,
Madison demolished the position of Washington and the Federalists:

> But, after all, whatever veneration might be entertained for the body
> of men who formed our Constitution, the sense of that body could
> never be regarded as the oracular guide in expounding the Constitu-
> tion. As the instrument came from them it was nothing more than the
> draft of a plan, nothing but a dead letter, until life and validity were
> breathed into it by the voice of the people, speaking through the
> several State Conventions. If we were to look, therefore, for the
> meaning of the instrument beyond the face of the instrument, we
> must look for it, not in the General Convention, which proposed, but
> in the State Conventions, which accepted and ratified the Constitu-
> tion.[36]

An examination of the proceedings of the state conventions supported
the position of the Republicans. It was the same issue Madison had addressed in the pamphlet battle with Hamilton over presidential power
to proclaim neutrality. But this time the Republican forces were much

stronger. Not only was the pride of the House involved,—a motive which cut cleanly across the party line,—but the Jay Treaty itself was unpopular with a good many Federalists.

Madison's resolution, introduced by Thomas Blount of North Carolina, took the position, in reply to Washington, that the House laid no claim to a share in the making of treaties, "but that when a treaty stipulates regulations on any of the subjects submitted by the Constitution to the power of Congress, it must depend for its execution, as to such stipulations, on a law or laws to be passed by Congress." Thus it was not only the right but the duty of the House, in all such cases, "to deliberate on the expediency or inexpediency of carrying such treaty into effect. . . ."[37] The Republicans carried this resolution, again by a substantial majority, and thus won the second round. Though they did not succeed, by this means, in repudiating the Jay Treaty, they did establish a principle of major importance for the conduct of American foreign relations. As Henry Adams points out, when a similar question was raised at the time of the annexation of Alaska the executive conceded the power of Congress without a struggle. It has long since become the practice of the executive to keep the House leadership well informed in all questions of treaty provisions which might call for appropriations or enabling legislation. Among other devices, joint Congressional resolutions, in advance of important treaty or other international negotiations, have become customary to provide the executive with indications of the support or non-support it may expect. While the jealousies of the various branches of government continue to flourish, no one any longer doubts the power of the House to review the merits of international agreements it is called upon to support by legislation.

The principled victory the Republicans thus achieved, gave them their opportunity to attack the merits of the Jay Treaty itself. Madison argued that it failed to secure agreement to the principle that "free ships make free goods," and so undermined the law of nations. Gallatin and Madison both denounced it as pusillanimous in the face of continued British depredations on American shipping and the impressment of American seamen. The article which allowed the British to declare provisions contraband was attacked as both contrary to the law of nations and a betrayal of American obligations to France. In sum, the Republicans undertook to show that the treaty had the effect of throwing the United States into the balance on the British side in the European war, at the expense of republican principles and without any offsetting advantages. But the climate of opinion was shifting rapidly, and fear of the British consolidated the Federalist ranks. Madison and Gallatin tried vainly to discount the danger of war. "The idea of war, as a consequence of refusing to give effect to the treaty," Madison told the House, "was too visionary and incredible to be admitted into the question. No man would say that the United States, if an independent people, had not a right to judge of their own interests, and to decline any treaty that did not duly provide for them."[38] Gallatin spoke even more sharply:

> I cannot help considering the cry of war, the threats of a dissolution of government, and the present alarm, as designed for the same purpose, that of making an impression on the fears of this House. It was through the fear of being involved in a war that the negotiation with Great Britain originated; under the impression of fear the treaty has been negotiated and signed; a fear of the same danger, that of war, promoted its ratification: and now every imaginary mischief which can alarm our fears is conjured up, in order to deprive us of that discretion which this House thinks it has a right to exercise, and in order to force us to carry the treaty into effect.[39]

But even such leadership proved inadequate, and the growing fear spread to the Republican side. "A few wrong heads," wrote Madison to Jefferson, "thought fit to separate, whereby the motion was lost by one vote." He was referring to a last ditch maneuver to accept the treaty but to add a condemnatory preamble. Thus the Republicans lost, in the final round, the most sustained and bitter foreign policy battle of their days in opposition. But, as in many other matters of both domestic and foreign policy, their logical consistency and moral commitment to republicanism brought about the establishment of an enduring principle which broadened the popular base of government in the United States.

It was in this atmosphere of Republican defeat and widespread fear of Britain that Monroe returned to America and published his *A View of the Conduct of the Executive, in the Foreign Affairs of the United States, connected with the Mission to the French Republic, during the Years 1794, 1795, and 1796*. This work, which was fully endorsed by Jefferson, Madison, Gallatin, and other Republican leaders, deserves special attention. It not only exhibits the record of Monroe's mission as he himself saw it, but contains many useful expressions of Republican principle and policy. In the latter aspect it rises well above the usual level of party polemics and helps to mark off the distinctive contributions of the Republicans to the formulation of a democratic foreign policy. The bitterness with which it was received by the Federalists—

"it will have no impression beyond the circle of Tom Paine's admirers," wrote Oliver Wolcot to Washington[40]—only emphasized Jefferson's contention that it "bites." Washington annotated his copy quite fully, sometimes effectively, but always irascibly.[41]

Monroe begins with an account of the circumstances surrounding his appointment. He reviews the record to show that his Republican affiliation was universally understood, not least by the administration, and to indicate that the chief factor in his appointment must have been the fact that he was a Republican. He recalls his opposition to the appointment of Gouverneur Morris, his predecessor at Paris, and makes the ground of his objection to Jay abundantly clear. "I also thought, from a variety of considerations, it would be difficult to find within the limits of the United States, a person who was more likely to improve, to the greatest possible extent, the mischief to which the measure [a special mission to England] naturally exposed us."[42] He reminded the Secretary of State of his position, and was assured, he says, "that my political principles, which were known to favor the French Revolution and to cherish a friendly connection with France, were a strong motive with the President for offering me the mission, since he wished to satisfy the French government what his own sentiments were upon those points." He then gives a detailed account of his instructions from Randolph and of the documents which he took with him expressing the official American view of France. This whole opening portion is so constructed as to draw the sharpest possible contrast between his own mission and Jay's and to question the sincerity of the administration in sending him at all.

Monroe next gives a documented narrative of his conduct in Paris, which began with a strong suggestion that the French government suspected that his mission was a cover for the negotiations in London. He learned unofficially why the Committee of Public Safety delayed recognizing him for so long that he decided to address himself directly to the National Convention. "It was intimated to me that the committee, or several at least of its members, had imbibed an opinion that Mr. Jay was sent to England with views unfriendly to France, and that my mission to France was adopted for the purpose of covering and supporting his to England; that the one was a measure of substantial import, contemplating on our part a close union with England; and that the other was an act of policy, intended to amuse and deceive." The obstacle thus presented was obviated by the device of going directly to the Convention. And from that point affairs proceeded well for several months. In spite of rumors that Jay's treaty contained matters not authorized, so far as

Monroe knew, and unfriendly to France, he succeeded in restoring American-French relations to the condition they had been in when Jefferson left Paris in 1789. In short, he managed to undo all the mischief Morris had done. In the latter part of 1794 and the early months of 1795, the French government agreed to recognize the claims of American merchants for losses sustained by the Bordeaux embargo, to suspend restrictions against American commerce, to recognize the principle that "free ships make free goods," to honor the commercial agreements of the Treaty of 1778, and even to allow American ships to become the carriers of England and her allies in the war. "In short," says Monroe, "such was our situation with the French Republic, and with other powers, so far as depended on the French Republic, that there was but one point upon which we had cause to feel or express any solicitude, which was that it might not vary." To these successes were to be added, later on, the securing of French aid, through her treaty with Spain, in freeing the Mississippi for navigation, and even an offer to secure and turn the Floridas over to the United States.

Next Monroe turns his attention to his relation with Jay and his efforts to obtain the text of the treaty. This portion of the book is seriously marred by Monroe's prejudice and by turgid writing. It is not, in fact, always clear whether Jay is guilty of a particular breach of good faith at a particular time, as Monroe suggests, or whether both men were victims of faulty and delayed communication. What is certain, however, is that Monroe did not get the treaty itself until it was too late to give the French the sort of friendly and disarming account of it he had hoped to be able to give, and that the treaty gave the lie to what he had in fact said. "It appeared that Mr. Jay had concluded a treaty upon other principles than those to which his powers were restricted, as inferred from my instructions, and of course, that the nature and object of his mission to England had been misrepresented, through me, to the French government." Thus, from the Republican viewpoint at least, Monroe's mission was ruined.

In the later portion of the book Monroe gives a vivid account of his conduct leading to his recall, the circumstances attending that clearly foreseen event, and more important, his estimate of the situation produced by his and Jay's missions in relation to proper policy for a free people. The procedure which led to the existing condition of affairs had, he thought, been systematic on the part of the administration. He sums up the matter in fourteen specific points, briefly as follows: 1) the appointment of Morris, a man known to be a friend of royalty and an enemy of the French Revolution; 2) continuing Morris in office until his recall was demanded by the French; 3) allowing it to be known that there was no disapproval of Morris's conduct; 4) his own appointment to Paris and Jay's to London, "from the apprehension those missions would produce, in our foreign relations, precisely the ill effect they did produce;" 5) the character of his instructions, which deliberately concealed the fact that Jay was to undertake a full-scale commercial treaty; 6) the assurances of American friendship to France, in contradiction to previous policy; 7) the resentment of the administration at his publication of those assurances; 8) the pressure on him to get the French government to repeal the decrees which hampered American commerce, and the deliberate ignoring of his achievement in getting them repealed; 9) giving Jay power to negotiate a commercial treaty with Britain without making similar overtures to France; 10) withholding the text of the Jay Treaty from Monroe so that he unwittingly gave false impressions to the French; 11) submitting the treaty to Mr. Adet, the French *chargé d'affaires*, to ask his opinion *after* it had been decided to ratify it; 12) the character of the treaty itself, which departs from the law of nations, prohibits provisions for France, and surrenders the principle that "free ships make free goods;" 13) the continued deliberate irritation of the French after the treaty had been signed; and 14) his recall precisely when he was preventing a rupture, indicating that a rupture with France was desired.

By contrast with this "system" of foreign policy, Monroe goes on to show what would have been the result of adhering to the French alliance. In terms of self-interest he marked out the advantages to American commerce which had already accrued by the treaty of 1778, the special advantage of protection to American ships carrying the goods of France's enemies while she was at war, and more beneficial arrangements for the future with a country "surpassing all others in the fertility and extent of her colonial possessions." But still more important, he thought, was the matter of principle:

> To stand well with France through the whole of this European war, was the true interest of America; since great advantage was to be derived from it in many views; and no injury in any. What would have been the condition of these States had France been conquered, and the coalesced powers triumphed, it is easy to perceive. Had the duke of Brunswick, for example reached Paris, and the kings of Europe, after distributing among themselves such portions of that flourishing country as suited each, dictated to the residue such form of

government as they pleased (if indeed they had not annihilated the name of France as they have done that of Poland) was it to be presumed that America, who, as the parent of liberty, was likewise the parent of the French Revolution, would have escaped their notice? Or was it likely that by a variance with France, preserving as we do, and I trust shall always preserve, our free elective government, that we should have stood well with them, hated as we know we are by one of the parties, who cannot view us in any other light than that of rebels?

Thus the principle that "republics should approach near to each other," which he had announced to the French Convention in 1794, would have insured the safety of American institutions, while, in view of the actual policy of the administration, it was no better than American good luck that France had been successful in arms and the kings of Europe were not free to turn against the United States.

In his conclusion Monroe makes a powerful restatement of the theme that liberty and republicanism should bind the peoples of the world for peace and prosperity:

We have heard much of intrigues, between the people of these States and the government of France. But free people seldom intrigue together; because there is no motive for it. Between the leaders however of a free people, and the neighboring monarchs, such intrigues often take place, and always will take place, whilst liberty is odious to monarchs, and men can be found base enough to betray her. If we read the history of the ancient Grecian republics, we shall see many examples of intrigues between the kings of Persia and the leaders of those republics; whilst none are to be seen of combinations between the people of any of those republics and the free governments of another, except for the purpose of overthrowing their tyrants.

And, finally, he characterizes the plight of America in the blackest terms. The vision of a union of the free, commenced by a close association with France, must give place to a bitter actuality in which "our national honor is in the dust; we have been kicked, cuffed, and plundered all over the ocean; our reputation for faith scouted; our government and people branded as cowards, incapable of being provoked to resist, and ready to receive again those chains we had taught others to burst. Long will it be before we shall be able to forget what we are, nor will centuries suffice to raise us to the high ground from which we have fallen."

If this kind of language seems both intemperate and unjustified, it may be well to remember what the actual conditions were. French reaction to the Jay Treaty had brought the beginning of the "undeclared war" with France which plagued John Adams's administration; the British depredations continued unabated; and at home the most dangerous threat to the civil liberties was already under way and issued only a year later in the Alien and Sedition Acts. Under such circumstances the Republicans saw liberty fading out of reach and their dream of the republic of the free collapsing. They were looked upon as subversive and disloyal, as fear became the paramount emotion.

Under modern methods of conducting foreign affairs the kind of disloyalty of which Monroe was guilty could scarcely take place. The hunt for subversives which characterizes the nineteen-fifties is of a different order. While Communists may attempt to infiltrate the foreign as well as any other service of the government, no President of this day would think of appointing an avowed political enemy to a position where his politics would inevitably direct his conduct against the policy of the administration. The enduring lesson of Monroe's mission, a lesson which the Republicans well learned, was that deep partisan differences must be recognized for what they are—expressions of freedom—and eliminated from responsible administrative action. The majority party must accept full responsibility for its policy, and the opposition, remaining out of power until it can command the majority, must be content to criticize.[43]

The future, for more than a century, turned out to be less dark than Monroe envisioned it. But many years of bitter tension and anxiety and a major war had to be endured before there could emerge the daylight of an "era of good feeling"—in his own administration. And in the perspective of the more than one hundred and fifty years since his recall from Paris, we do not appear often to have reached again "the high ground from which we have fallen."

V

It is not necessary here to concern ourselves with developments in foreign relations during the years after Monroe returned from Paris, and, in any case, no period in American history has been more fully treated than that from the "undeclared war" with France through the War of 1812. In general, it is enough to observe that the Republicans maintained their principles of avoiding political entanglements and of striving for freedom of the seas until the bitter end, when war with Britain seemed no longer to be escaped. Even the purchase of Louisiana in 1803 involved no departure from principle. But, as commercial relations with Britain deteriorated towards open warfare, the Republicans achieved a further formulation of the principle that "free ships make free goods" which rounded out their theory and made a lasting contribution to American foreign policy. The vehicle was Madison's treatise on neutral commerce which, as Secretary of State, he prepared in the summer of 1806.

A Memoir containing an Examination of the British Doctrine which subjects to Capture a Neutral Trade not open in Time of Peace was an informal report presented by Madison to the closing session of the Ninth Congress. It was a document of remarkable scope and profound scholarship, argued with all of its author's familiar skill at legal interpretation. Thirty years later, in his eulogy of Madison, John Quincy Adams asserted that it "will hereafter be considered a standard Treatise on the Law of Nations, not inferior to the works of any writer upon those subjects since the day of Grotius."[44]

The situation to which Madison addressed himself was brought about by British depredations on American commerce incident to the European war. The practices of search, seizure, and impressment had been more and more characteristic of British behavior since 1793, and, as we have seen, the Jay Treaty of 1794 had involved the United States, over the stubborn opposition of the Republicans, in something like recognition of this behavior as a right, by allowing the British to seize provisons for France as contraband. Madison formulated the problem in this way:

> . . . every belligerent right to control neutral commerce must, as an exception to the general freedom of commerce, be positively and strictly proved, and the more strictly, as the exceptions are in a course of restriction rather than extension, [therefore] the question is ready for examination, whether it be a part of the law of nations, that a trade ordinarily shut in time of peace, and opened to neutrals in time of war, on account of the war, is liable, as much as a trade in contraband of war or with a blockaded port, to capture and condemnation.[45]

He makes three separate approaches to the problem: 1) by examining the writings of the received authorities on the law of nations, 2) by examining the well-known treaties of the preceding one hundred and fifty or more years, and 3) by analyzing the development of the British doctrine in British admiralty courts. In accordance with the convention of his time, he assumes that the "oracles," treaties, and court judgments together constitute the "law of nations," which, in general terms, he defines as follows:

[the law of nations] consists of those rules of conduct which reason deduces, as consonant to justice and common good, from the nature of the society existing among independent nations; with such definitions and modifications as may be established by general consent.[46]

The law of nations as Madison thus formulates it was, despite its long evolution, a characteristic doctrine of the Enlightenment. Like the Lockian version of the contract theory of government to which the Republicans adhered, it assumes the priority of "reason" among the sanctions for human action. It assumes also that peoples and nations wish to reconcile liberty with order and to do so by discovering and conforming to the "laws of nature." Thus the law is devoted to the advancement of "civilization," and to peace as the necessary condition for human progress. In practice, therefore, belligerents normally appealed to the exceptions to the law of nations, while neutrals appealed to its general principles and peaceful intentions. This latter was Madison's method, as he undertook to show that the British were distorting even the exceptions, and that the American position was supported by the plain intent of the law.

In the first portion of his study Madison draws copiously on Grotius, Pufendorf, Bynkershoeck, Vattel and Martens to show a) that neutral rights are not obviated by a state of war, b) that exceptions are to be justified by necessity only, and c) that exceptions include only contraband and trade with a blockaded or besieged port. Thus Grotius:

It may seem needless for us to treat of those that are not engaged in war, when *it is manifest that the right of war cannot affect them:* but because upon occasion of war, many things are done against them *on pretence of necessity;* it may be proper here to repeat what we have already mentioned before, that the necessity must be *really extreme,* to give any right to another's goods: that it is requisite that the proprietor be not himself in the like necessity. When real necessity urges us to take, we should then take no more that what it requires; that is, if the bare keeping of it be enough, we ought to leave the use of it to the proprietor; and if the use be necessary, we ought not to consume it; and if we cannot help consuming it, we ought to return the full value of it.[47]

Madison also calls upon Grotius for authority on the behavior of neutrals toward belligerents. The neutral powers should take care not to advance the interests of a nation having "an ill cause," while if the merits of the war are "dubious," neutrals should "behave themselves alike to both parties." This is precisely the policy of the United States which is being interrupted by Britain.

Next Madison appeals to Pufendorf, but finds that the great Swiss gave little attention to the problem. It is true that he showed more concern than Grotius had done for the claims of belligerents under the motive of necessity, but in his letter to Groningius it is clear that he is only describing the actual behavior of certain nations at war, not condoning it—"The laws of humanity and equity between nations do not extend so far as to require, *without any apparent necessity*, that one people should give up its profit in favor of another."[48] British jurists have made full use of Pufendorf in defense of their position, but this is accomplished only by attributing views to Pufendorf which he is quoting from others by way of illustration. The whole weight of his authority, on the contrary, is behind the doctrine of freedom of the seas.

In important respects Bynkershoeck is Madison's best authority. He quotes him at length and then summarizes the position:

> He lays it down as a general rule, that the trade of neutrals with the nations at war, provided it be impartial, is as if there were no war; but that certain articles, as instruments of war, form an exception to this general rule; to which he suggests as a further exception, the case of a siege, or of a similar pressure of famine. It cannot be pretended that there is either a single general expression, or particular allusion, that can be tortured into an exception of any trade, merely for the British reason, that it was not open to neutrals before, as well as during, the war.[49]

Bynkershoeck, further, defends the rights of neutrals by showing that an intent of impartiality is adequate, in view of the fact that certain normal trade relations will inevitably favor one of two belligerents more than the other. Such trade is not to be interrupted by the less favored nation, unless under the exceptions already noted.

Vattel, to whom Madison next appeals, makes the same point, but carries it considerably further. Thus, while neutrals are bound by the rule of impartiality, they retain their sovereign right to consult their own self-interest above all else. Unlike the other authorities, Vattel moves out of the strict realm of commerce to observe that private citizens retain the right to loan money to one or the other of two belligerents on a basis of preference.

Vattel, Madison points out, is an especially valuable court of appeal since he is more frequently and favorably cited by the British than any other. In spite of a certain lack of lucidity in his style and definitions, he can readily be shown to stand firmly with his predecessors on the whole question under discussion. The following passage is representative:

It is certain that, as they [neutrals] have no part in my quarrel, they are under no obligation to abandon their trade that they may avoid furnishing my enemy with the means of making war. Should they make it a point not to sell to me any of these articles, whilst they take measures for transporting great quantities of them to my enemy, with a manifest intention of favoring him, such a *partiality* would exclude them from the neutrality they enjoyed. But if they simply pursue their commerce they do not *thereby declare themselves* against my interest; they only exercise a right, which they are under no obligation of sacrificing to me.[50]

Vattel goes on, in the usual manner, to make exceptions under "the law of necessity." But these are the same exceptions we have hitherto encountered. Nowhere does he, or any of the others, except a neutral trade made possible by the fact of a war. Indeed he specifically asserts that the doctrine of necessity, as it harms a friendly neutral, may not be carried beyond a certain point. "But that *limits* may be set to these inconveniences; that the commerce of neutral nations may subsist in all the freedom which the laws of war will admit, these are rules to be observed, and on which *Europe seems to be generally agreed.*[51]

Finally Madison calls to witness the German jurist Martens—and does so with relish. For Martens was a professor in the university at Hanover and drew his salary from the English king as Elector of Hanover. However, he has been severely attacked by British jurists precisely because his stand on the question of neutral trade is so unequivocal. "The right that a nation enjoys in time of peace of selling and carrying all sorts of merchandize to every nation *who chooses to trade* with it, it enjoys also in time of war, provided that it remains neutral." And further, "since a belligerent power cannot exercise hostilities in a neutral place, nor confiscate property belonging to neutral subjects, such power ought not to confiscate the goods of an enemy found in a neutral vessel navigating on a free or neutral sea, nor neutral goods found in the vessel of an enemy; provided, however, in both cases that these goods are not warlike stores."[52]

The force of the conclusion is direct. The received authorities on the law of nations are unanimous in their assertion of neutral rights to trade with belligerents, except in contraband of war or at besieged or blockaded ports. At no point do they make an exception of a neutral trade brought about by war. The whole weight of testimony contradicts the

British view. And it is against this background that Madison proceeds to examine the evidence to be found in treaties.

First he establishes the bearing which treaties are agreed to have upon the law of nations:

They may be considered as simply repeating or affirming the general law: they may be considered as making exceptions to the general law, which are to be a particular law between the parties themselves: they may be considered as explanatory of the law of nations, on points where its meaning is otherwise obscure or unsettled; in which case they are, first, a law between the parties themselves, and next, a sanction to the general law, according to the reasonableness of the explanation, and the number and character of the parties to it: lastly, treaties may be considered as constituting a voluntary or positive law.[53]

With meticulous attention to each of these relations Madison then examines the provisions of more than thirty treaties, from 1648 to the time of writing, including such historic documents as those of Westphalia, Utrecht, Aix la Chappelle, Paris (1763), and Paris (1783). To some of these Britain was a party, and Madison draws appropriate comparisons between what the British themselves have agreed to and what other nations have thought proper without reference to them. He accumulates the evidence gradually and inevitably, until the reader is nearly borne down by its weight. There is simply no precedent for the British insistence on their special exception to the rights of neutrals and the freedom of the seas. "It may be confidently affirmed," Madison says at the outset of this phase of the inquiry, "that on no point ever drawn into question, the evidence of treaties was more uniform, more extensive, or more satisfactory."[54] When he has finished, the reader can only mutter a weak Amen.

There remains the evidence to be drawn from the British courts. It is here that Madison excels in the art of convicting an opponent out of his own mouth. He shows, with copious quotation and a dry minimum of commentary, that until recent years British judges have faithfully adhered to the accepted law of nations in their awards of damages and their determinations of proper procedure. Only since the outbreak of the war with France have they begun to recognize the right of their navy to seize and confiscate on the high seas either ships or cargoes in neutral trade incident to war. But, what is worse, these recent decisions, attempting to re-write the law of nations, deal almost uniformly with cases involving the United States. As Madison shows earlier, a treaty of

1801 with Russia had reaffirmed Britain's acceptance of the principle that only contraband of war or commerce with a blockaded or besieged port was subject to interference by a neutral. Yet from the outset of American independence, and with ever-growing boldness, the British have applied their new and unexampled principle to the United States. In fact it may be said that they have never actually recognized American independence and sovereignty at all. "Would Great Britain be patient under such proceedings against her, if she held in her hands, the means of controlling them? If she will not answer for herself, all the world will answer for her, that she would not, and what is more, that she ought not."[55]

At least three paramount implications are to be drawn from Madison's treatise. *First*, by identifying American policy with the universally accepted principles of maritime countries, he effectively isolates Great Britain, leaving her in the role of a cunning outlaw whose departures from the rule of reason and equity pit her against the whole moral force of that civilization which the law of nations is intended to advance. *Second*, he builds such firm moral and legal defenses for the position of the United States that the justice of the American cause against Britain in the War of 1812 can hardly be denied. Historians and statesmen have never ceased to question the wisdom of Madison's call for the declaration of that war. They have adduced the ambitions of the "War Hawks" (i.e. the "New Republicans" like Calhoun, Crawford, and Clay), the disaffection of New England merchants and shipbuilders, the weakness of American naval forces, the might of Britain and American need for her friendship, as well as other considerations, in order to denounce the war as folly or, at the very least, an ill-calculated adventure. But no one has disproved the validity of Madison's thesis. And *third*, Madison so thoroughly establishes the doctrine of the freedom of the seas—building on the older Republican principle that free ships make free goods— that, as John Quincy Adams suggested in 1836, his book provided a kind of charter for later American Presidents and Secretaries of State, until the British practice of naval searches made it in part obsolete. While Americans of the twentieth century have doubtless paid little heed to Madison or his *Examination*, his language and spirit are none the less adumbrated in Woodrow Wilson's war message of April 2, 1917; his formulations of the rights of neutrals were not irrelevant to the American problem at the beginning of the Second World War; nor, perhaps, are they irrelevant to the complex problem of the present.

VI

Though it postdated by many years the period in which Republican principles and doctrines were established and elaborated, the Monroe Doctrine marked a kind of fruition of Republican thought in the field of foreign policy, so that it may properly be considered here in that context. In Monroe's historic pronouncement of December 2, 1823 are combined two primary Republican precepts—Jefferson's insistence on avoiding political entanglements with the Old World, and Monroe's own principle that "republics should approach near to each other." It was a kind of poetic propriety that Jefferson, Madison, and Gallatin should all have contributed, at so late a day, to Monroe's formulation, and it was fitting, as well, that the son of John Adams should have played a principal part.

The moral and theoretical background of the Monroe Doctrine is admirably drawn by John Quincy Adams in his instructions, as Secretary of State, to Richard Anderson on the latter's appointment to be Minister to the new republic of Colombia. Speaking of the revolutions in Latin America, Adams observes, "As a general movement in human affairs, it is, perhaps, no more than a development of principles first brought into action by the separation of these states from Great Britain, and by the practical illustration given in the formation and establishment of our Union to the doctrine that voluntary agreement is the only legitimate source of authority among men, and that all just government is a compact."[56] He recognizes, of course, that the independence of South American republics from Europe is owing to different causes, but the United States will treat the result with a consistently republican attitude:

> Their [the Americans'] policy, their interest and their feelings, all concurred to favor the cause of the colonies; and the principles upon which the right of independence has been maintained by South American patriots have been approved, not only as identical with those upon which our own independence was asserted and achieved, but as involving the whole theory of government on the emphatically American foundation of the sovereignty of the people, and the unalienable rights of man. To a cause reposing upon this basis, the people of this country never could be indifferent, and their sympathies have accordingly been with great unanimity and constancy enlisted in its favor. The sentiments of the government of the United States have been in perfect harmony with those of their people; and which

forbearing, as their duties of neutrality prescribed, from every measure which could justly be construed as hostile to Spain, they have exercised all the moral influence which they possessed to countenance and promote the cause of independence.[57]

But the Americans were under no illusion, as they has once been in the case of France, that the principles of republican liberty would have an easy triumph. Monroe himself, in a letter to Jefferson, spoke of the difficulties. "The great defect," he said, "is the ignorance of the people, by means whereof, they are made, in the hands of military adventurers, and priests, the instruments of their own destruction. Time, however, with some internal convulsions, and the form of our example, will gradually mature them, for the great trust deposited in their hands."[58] Adams stressed this point in his instructions to Anderson, paying particular heed to the fact that Latin Americans were adherents of an authoritarian church:

Religious and military coercion will be alike discarded from all the institutions framed for the protection of human rights in civil society of independent nations; and the freedom of opinion and of faith will be guaranteed by the same sanctions as the rights to personal liberty and security. To promote this event by all the moral influence which we can exercise by our example is among the duties which devolve upon us in the formation of our future relations with our southern neighbors; and in the intercourse which is hereafter to subsist between us, as their citizens who may visit or transiently reside with us, will enjoy the benefit of religious freedom in its utmost latitude, we are bound to claim for our countrymen who may occasionally dwell for a time with them, the reciprocal exercise of the same natural rights.[59]

The political situation was like a providential dispensation to permit the marriage of republican idealism with American national interest. The wars in Europe were destroying Spain as a world power, and at the same time detaching Britain from the coalition of kings. Gallatin, back from Paris, reported to Secretary Adams that France had disclaimed any intention to interfere in South America after he had informed Chateaubriand that "if France was successful in her attack on Spain, and afterwards attempted either to take possession of some of her colonies or to assist her in reducing them under her former yoke, I was of the opinion that the United States would oppose every undertaking of this kind, and it might force them into an alliance with Great Britain."[60] He had likewise taken occasion to advise the Russian minister to France that Russia would do well to deny herself the temptation to establish more colonies in the Americas. The minister "seemed to coincide with me in opinion." In October Monroe sent to Jefferson two letters from Canning, the British Foreign Secretary, proposing co-operation between Great Britain and the United States against the designs of the Holy Alliance upon South America. Thus the opportunity was perfected, and Monroe asked Jefferson's advice on American policy, first setting forth his own opinion:

My own impression is that we ought to meet the proposal of the British government and make it known, that we would view an interference on the part of the European powers, and especially an attack on the colonies, by them, as an attack on ourselves, presuming that, if they succeeded with them, they would extend it to us.[61]

Jefferson's reply is nearly as famous as Monroe's message, and is worth quoting at length:

The question presented by the letters you have sent me, is the most momentous which has ever been offered to my contemplation since that of independence. That made us a nation, this sets our compass and points the course which we are to steer through the ocean of time opening on us. And never could we embark on it under circumstances more auspicious. Our first and fundamental maxim should be, never to entangle ourselves in the broils of Europe. Our second, never to suffer Europe to intermeddle with cis-Atlantic affairs. America, North and South, has a set of interests distinct from those of Europe, and peculiarly her own. She should therefore have a system of her own, separate and apart from that of Europe. While the last is laboring to become the domicile of despotism, our endeavor should surely be, to make our hemisphere that of freedom. One nation, most of all, could disturb us in this pursuit; she now offers to lead, aid, and accompany us in it. By acceding to her proposition, we detach her from the bands, bring her mighty weight into the scale of free government, and emancipate a continent at one stroke, which might otherwise linger long in doubt and difficulty.[62]

He goes on to say that the United States should "most sedulously cherish a cordial friendship" with Britain; even to fight in the same cause with her, if that should be necessary to enforce the new position. But he thought, rather, that it was a policy of peace, and if war should eventuate, it would be "ours," not one of Britain's European squabbles.

Madison, to whom Monroe also applied for advice, took the same view, though he expressed it with characteristic reserve. "The professions we have made to these neighbors, our sympathies with their liberties and independence, the deep interest we have in the most friendly relations with them, and the consequences threatened by a command of their resources by the Great Powers confederated against the rights and reforms, of which we have given so conspicuous and persuasive an example," all these, Madison wrote, "unite in calling for our efforts to defeat the meditated crusade." As for the role of Great Britain, it was particularly fortunate that her policy, "though guided by calculations different from ours, has presented a co-operation for an object the same with ours."[63]

When President Monroe delivered his message to the Congress he made no mention of America's dependence on Britain for the implementation of the new policy. But everyone knew how it had come about. In foreign policy the Republican wheel had come full around. It is ironic, perhaps, but satisfying that the ancient enemy in the struggle for liberty, the symbol of monarchy and oppression against whom the Republicans had always directed their sharpest weapons, should become the permanent ally. There was no treaty with Britain in 1823, only the plain declaration of the principle "in which the rights and interests of the United States are involved, that the American continents, by the free and independent condition they have assumed and maintain, are henceforth not to be considered as subjects for future colonization by any European powers."[64] But Castlereagh and Canning, as well as Monroe and Jefferson, Madison, Gallatin, and John Quincy Adams must be honored by free men of the twentieth century as founders of an alliance which, in a far different world, remains the best hope of man for freedom, dignity, and peace.

NOTES

1. Monroe, *Writings*, II, 13.
2. Madison, *Writings*, VI, 88, (2 February, 1792).
3. *Ibid.*, 89-90.
4. *Ibid.*
5. *Ibid.*
6. *Ibid.*, 90-91.
7. Jefferson, *Writings*, VI, 220.
8. *Ibid.*, 221.
9. For Taylor's views on free trade see E. Mudge, *The Social Philosophy of John Taylor of Caroline*, 1937, pp. 186 ff.
10. Jefferson, *Writings*, VI, 220.
11. *Ibid.*, 231.
12. Madison, *Writings*, VI, 128, (8 May, 1793).
13. *Ibid.*, 127, (10 June, 1793).

14. Monroe, *Writings,* I, 269, (23 July, 1793).
15. *Ibid.,* 262, (27 June, 1793).
16. Jefferson, *Writings,* VI, 338. This letter is a dramatic example of the way in which party spirit operated, i.e. *inside* the administration, as Washington tried futilely to check it. The normal American practice, of government by one party with opposition by the other, may be said to have begun after Jefferson's retirement at the end of 1793, but was not regularized until John Adams's administration.
17. Madison, *Writings,* VI, 139-140.
18. *Ibid.,* 142-143.
19. *Ibid.,* 141, (11 August, 1793).
20. *Ibid.,* 145.
21. *Ibid.,* 150.
22. *Ibid.,* 151.
23. Jefferson, *Writings,* VI, 479. *Report on the Privileges and Restrictions on the Commerce of the United States in Foreign Countries,* 11 December, 1793.
24. *Ibid.,* 480.
25. Madison, *Writings,* VI, 206.
26. Monroe, *Writings,* I, 289.
27. *Ibid.,* 291-292.
28. The instructions are given entire in Monroe's *Writings,* II, 1-9.
29. *Ibid.,* 13-15.
30. *Ibid.,* footnote p. 15.
31. *Ibid.,* 50.
32. *Ibid.,* 64.
33. See *Writings,* II, from the beginning of 1795, *passim.*
34. Adams, *Life of Gallatin,* 186-187.
35. *Ibid.,* 161.
36. Madison, *Writings,* VI, 272.
37. *Ibid.,* 264.
38. *Ibid.,* 295.
39. Adams, *Life of Gallatin,* 165.
40. 20 January, 1797. Quoted in Monroe, *Writings,* III, 385-386.
41. Washington, *Writings,* ed. J. C. Fitzpatrick, XXXVI, 194-237.
42. Monroe, *Writings,* III, 386. Quotations from *A View* are all taken from the text in this edition, 383-457.
43. "In the light of after events, Monroe's attempt to represent the people rather than the government of the United States appears to have constituted the real reason for his removal. The private correspondence of Pickering with the President points to a like conclusion." B. W. Bond, "The Monroe Mission to France, 1794-1796", *Johns Hopkins University Studies in Historical and Political Science,* XXV, 1907, 78-79.
44. *Selected Writings of John and John Quincy Adams,* ed. Koch and Peden, 1946., 385.
45. Madison, *Writings,* (Congress edition), 1884, II, 232.
46. *Ibid.,* 262.

47. *Ibid.*, 234-235. The italics are Madison's, as in all subsequent quotations from the authorities.
48. *Ibid.*, 241.
49. *Ibid.*, 245.
50. *Ibid.*, 251.
51. *Ibid.*, 252.
52. *Ibid.*, 254-255.
53. *Ibid.*, 260.
54. *Ibid.*, 261.
55. *Ibid.*, 391.
56. Adams, *op. cit.*, 345.
57. *Ibid.*, 346.
58. Monroe, *Writings*, VI, 317-318, (18 August, 1823).
59. Adams, *op. cit.*, 348.
60. Gallatin to J. Q. Adams, (24 June, 1823). Quoted in Monroe, *Writings* VI, 315.
61. *Ibid.*, 324-325.
62. Jefferson, *Writings*, X, 214.
63. Madison, *Writings*, IX, 157-158.
64. Monroe, *Writings*, XI, 382.

It is error alone which needs the support of government. Truth can stand by itself.

— Thomas Jefferson, 1781.

CHAPTER FIVE
Religion and the State

THE CHARACTERISTICALLY American doctrines of the free conscience and the separation of church and state have had a long and frequently dramatic historical evolution. Many men, many events, and many writings have contributed to their development and gradual realization. The end, perhaps, is not yet. But the achievement is so substantial that in certain respects it transcends all others in the American experiment.[1] Neither religious attitudes nor the relation between church and state were directly at issue as between the Republicans and the Federalists. But the roles played by certain of the Republican leaders, notably Mason, Madison, and Jefferson, were so crucial as to justify special consideration in a study of the old Republican Party.

The new United States had a mixed religious inheritance from colonial days. While state established churches, as well as laws against impiety and heresy, prevailed in the South and in northern states like Massachusetts and Connecticut, other states like Rhode Island, Pennsylvania, and New York had already long traditions of religious freedom. Rhode Island, since its beginning, had been faithful to the radical example of Roger Williams; New York had repealed all restrictive laws; and Pennsylvania had been dominated not only by the Quakers but by Quaker forbearance. But these states had had little influence on their neighbors, and, as Stokes repeatedly says, it was the *political* achievement of the Virginia Republicans which was translated into national policy and set the national course. It is no accident that Madison, not Roger Williams or the Pennsylvania Quakers, should be cited in twentieth-century Supreme Court decisions dealing with freedom of conscience or the relation of church to state.

Although the states of the new Union differed sharply among themselves both in tradition and practice, they had common legal ground in the British Toleration Act of 1689, and a common area of discourse in Locke's theory as expressed in his *Letter Concerning Toleration*. Massachusetts may serve as a case in point. The second article of the Massachusetts Bill of Rights, written by John Adams in 1780, deals at length with the question of religion. It opens with the assertion that while it is "the duty of all men in society, publicly, and at stated seasons, to worship the Supreme Being," nevertheless "no subject shall be hurt, molested, or restrained, in his person, liberty, or estate, for worshipping God in the manner and season most agreeable to the dictates of his own conscience."[2] But the freedom thus declared is immediately restricted to believers, as the next paragraph makes clear:

As the happiness of a people and the good order and preservation of civil government essentially depend upon piety, religion, and morality, and as these cannot be generally diffused through a community but by the institution of the public worship of God and of public instructions, in piety, religion, and morality. Therefore to promote their happiness and secure the good order and preservation of their government, the people of this commonwealth have a right to invest their legislature with power to authorize and require, and the legislature shall from time to time authorize and require, the several towns . . . and other bodies politic or religious societies, to make suitable provision, at their own expense, for the institution of the public worship of God and the support and maintenance of public Protestant teachers of piety, religion, and morality. . . .[3]

Thus the Congregational churches are to be established by the power of the legislature, and the safety of the government itself is asserted to be dependent upon the establishment. But the Bill goes further: "And the people of this commonwealth . . . do invest their legislature with authority to enjoin upon all subjects an attendance upon the instructions of the public teachers aforesaid. . . ." The dictates of the citizen's own conscience are now reduced to the value of a literary expression. The citizen must worship God, must pay to support ministers and teachers, and must attend services and instruction. The ministers and teachers are to be Protestant, so that not only are all citizens restricted in their religious rights, but Jews, Catholics, members of other religious groups, and nonbelievers are to be required by law to violate their conscientious "dictates." Although the final paragraph of the article declares that every denomination "of Christians ... shall be equally under the protection of the law; and no subordination of any one sect or denomination to another shall ever be established by law," the restraints upon this freedom have already been set up in the controlling context.

This Massachusetts doctrine involves an adherence to the old Puritan tradition of an identity between church and state, but modified by the principle of toleration. Locke himself was concerned with the freedom of dissenters, while in Massachusetts the dissenters were established and Anglicans and others were to be protected. But the theory is the same. "Nobody, therefore, in fine, single persons nor churches, nay, nor even commonwealths, have any just title to invade the civil rights and worldly goods of each other upon pretence of religion."[4] Locke assumed, however, that the Christian religion was the true explanation of man's relation to God and that the Anglican Church was the true church of the Christian religion and should be established by the state. On the principles that the truth need not fear opposition and that force will not alter conscience, he concluded that the established church ought to tolerate dissent. But atheists were not worthy of toleration because their doctrines subverted the moral order, and Roman Catholics were also excepted as owing allegiance to a foreign prince. Thus Locke and Adams are in essential agreement. The whole philosophy depends upon the prior assumption that religious truth is known. This known truth is to be given institutional form, and the institution thus created is, within certain limits, to tolerate error. Such freedom as non-adherents of the established church may enjoy derives not from natural right but from the obligations of responsible authority. It is fair to add that the position of Roger Williams or of the Quakers differs only in the mode of formulation and in the degree of freedom allowed.[5]

The technique of the Virginia Republicans was to make use of the toleration theory as an accepted realm of discourse in order to attack its major premise. Their political achievement was to replace that premise with its obverse, i.e. that ultimate truth is not in any legal sense known. If it is not so known, it cannot be institutionalized, and there can be no agency to tolerate error. Thus religion is to be disengaged from the civil power, and toleration disappears in favor of freedom of conscience and thought, limited only by the secular welfare of the people.

Ten years were needed to bring about this radical departure from the Lockian tradition, ten years of studied reflection and political negotiation. The sequence begins with the drafting of the sixteenth article of the Virginia Declaration of Rights in June, 1776. George Mason, author of the first draft of the article, was a vestryman in the Episcopal Church and a firm believer. The Church had always been established by law, so that the primary problem was to determine its legal status after the separation from England. Mason's purposes were twofold— to retain the establishment, and to guarantee a broad interpretation of the toleration principle in the law. As he approached the problem, he appears not to have felt the presence of a contradiction between tolera- tion and freedom of conscience. In this regard his draft is not unlike that of John Adams. But he was equally anxious to see that no religious requirement would be imposed on the conduct of the citizens.

That as religion or the duty which we owe to our divine and omni- potent Creator, and the manner of discharging it, can be governed only by reason and conviction, not by force or violence; and there- fore that all men should enjoy the fullest toleration in the exercise of religion, according to the dictates of conscience, unpunished and un- restrained by the magistrate, unless, under color of religion, any man disturb the peace, the happiness, or safety of society, or of individuals. And that it is the mutual duty of all, to practice Christian forbear- ance, love and charity towards each other.[6]

Thus, like Adams, Mason identifies the "dictates of conscience" with freedom to worship as one pleases. But he goes much further by declar- ing a restraint upon the civil authority, as opposed to the Massachusetts pronouncement that the legislature is to require religious observances. But the basis of the draft is still the principle of toleration. Mason as- sumes that there is to be an official religion which will be bound to re- spect the rights of dissent.

In committee discussion, Madison, also an Episcopalian, undertook a revision of Mason's draft. Madison was only twenty-five at this time and was serving his first term in the Assembly. But he had been meditat- ing the problem of religious freedom since his college days at Princeton, where he had measured the Presbyterian orthodoxy of Witherspoon against that of the Anglicans in his home country, and concluded that all orthodoxies are dangerous. In a remarkable letter to his friend Wil- liam Bradford, in 1774, he speculated on the dangers that might come from religious uniformity:

If the Church of England had been established and general religion in all the northern colonies as it has been among us here, and unin- terrupted tranquility had prevailed throughout the continent, it is clear

to me that slavery and subjection might and would have been gradually insinuated among us. Union of religious sentiments begets a
surprising confidence, and ecclesiastical establishments tend to great
ignorance and corruption; all of which facilitate the execution of
mischievous projects.[7]

Madison had observed the weakness and corruption of the Anglican
clergy in Virginia, but, unlike Mason and others, he was unwilling to
assume that the Church would remain so weak under independence as
to offer no serious threat to religious freedom. In the same letter to
Bradford he speaks bitterly of persecutions for heresy in Virginia:

> That diabolical, hell-conceived principle of persecution rages among
> some; and to their eternal infamy, the clergy can furnish their quota
> of imps in such business. . . . There are at this time in the adjacent
> country not less than five or six well-meaning men in close jail for
> publishing their religious sentiments, which in the main are very or-
> thodox.

He goes on to tell his friend that he has "squabbled and scolded" about
these things for so long that he is out of patience, and closes the matter
by urging Bradford to "pity me, and pray for liberty of conscience to
all."[8]

He was in a less angry mood, assuredly, but moved by the same conviction, when he tackled Mason's draft in 1776. He wished to rid the
new state of any established religion and to do away with any form of
compulsion to religious worship. His draft was skillfully directed to
these ends:

> That religion or the duty we owe to our Creator, and the manner
> of discharging it, being under the direction of reason and conviction
> only, not of violence or compulsion, all men are equally entitled to
> the full and free exercise of it according to the dictates of conscience;
> and therefore that no man or class of men ought, on account of re-
> ligion to be invested with peculiar emoluments or privileges; nor
> subjected to any penalties or disabilities unless under color of religion,
> any man disturb the peace, the happiness, or safety of Society. And
> that it is the mutual duty of all to practice Christian forbearance,
> love, and charity, towards each other.[9]

This proposal involves three radical departures from Mason's original
draft. By substituting "compulsion" for "force" Madison hoped to deny
the civil government any power whatsoever to require religious observances. He excluded not only the word "toleration" but the whole
idea involved in it. And he sought to dis-establish the church by assert-

ing that no man should be "invested" with special status by reason of religion. Thus he agrees with Mason in resting the case for religion on "reason," but proceeds to draw the full logical implications from the premises. These were substantially greater steps than the committee, or the Assembly, were willing to take, and Madison was quickly forced to retreat. But his draft is none the less an important sign post on the road to the First Amendment to the Constitution.

Madison's political talent is well demonstrated, even at this early stage, by the manner in which, in his second attempt to revise Mason's article, he gave ground while still holding an advanced position. Since he had been defeated on three points, he decided to abandon two and try to regain a third. Of the three—prohibition of legal compulsion to religious worship, dis-establishment of the church, and removal of the principle of toleration— he saw that the third was crucial. If he could secure agreement to freedom of conscience on its own merits, the way would be open to ground the whole case on natural rather than civil right, and eventually both compulsion and the established church could be obviated. As Paine put it years later in *The Rights of Man*, Madison saw that "toleration is not the opposite of intolerance, but is the counterfeit of it. The one assumes to itself the right of withholding liberty of conscience, the other of granting it."[10] Thus by the expedient of restoring most of Mason's language, but omitting "toleration," he brought the committee and the Assembly to a far more radical position than had originally been intended, though there is reason to suppose that Mason himself understood and approved:

> That Religion or the duty we owe to our Creator, and the manner of discharging it, can be directed only by reason and conviction; not by force or violence; and therefore, that all men are equally entitled to the free exercise of religion, according to the dictates of conscience, unpunished, and unrestrained by the magistrate, unless the preservation of equal liberty and the existence of the State are manifestly endangered. And that it is the mutual duty of all, to practice Christian forbearance, love and charity towards each other.[11]

The key to this draft, as Brant puts it, is that "with the word 'toleration' eliminated, the 'dictates of conscience' became substantive, a fundamental right—no longer a mere definition of the extent to which freedom should be tolerated by those who rule the state, but the basis of men's inherent right to the free exercise of religion."[12] Mason accepted this version, as did the committee, but in the final form the clauses deal-

ing with the right of the civil government to interfere, if free worship
tended to subvert the state, were dropped as adequately provided for
in ordinary statutes against public disorder:

That religion, or the duty which we owe to our Creator, and the
manner of discharging it, can be directed only by reason and conviction, not by force or violence; and therefore all men are equally entitled to the free exercise of religion, according to the dictates of
conscience; and that it is the mutual duty of all to practice Christian
forbearance, love, and charity, towards each other.[13]

The next step of the Assembly was to enact legislation to implement
this article of the Declaration. Mason again was the principal drafts-
man, but the influence of Madison's position is clearly shown in the
way Mason approached the problem. It might, in short, be said that the
drafting of the article on religious freedom in the Declaration of Rights
was like the first encounter in a ten years' war, but it was the crucial
battle.

II

Though it recognized the establishment of the Episcopal Church, Mason's bill, which became Chapter II of the laws of Virginia under its
new constitution, was fully in accord with the Declaration of Rights.
The force of the law was to establish the church for its own members
only, by providing the fullest exemptions for dissenters. The title is
self-explanatory, "An act for exempting the different societies of Dissenters from contributing to the support and maintenance of the church
as by law established, and its ministers, and for other purposes. . . ."[14]
The precedent, of course, was the Toleration Act of 1689, but Mason
carried the principle further—indeed, as far as it would go.

The first provision was to repeal all acts of Parliament which had a
bearing on religious belief or practice: "That all and every act of Parliament, by whatever title known or distinguished, which renders criminal the maintaining any opinions in matters of religion, forbearing to
repair to church, or the exercising any mode of worship whatever, or
which prescribes punishments for the same, shall henceforth be of no
validity or force within this commonwealth." Thus, by statute, Virginia took exactly the opposite course from Massachusetts. Both acted
within the framework of the toleration theory, but Mason and Madison
were able to push to the outer limits of the theory, while Adams and
his colleagues were willing to remain at its center.

The second provision enacted the title of the law. It is important to notice that Mason grounded the exemption of dissenters upon "the principles of reason and justice." The act holds that it is contrary to these principles that "any should be compelled to contribute to the maintenance of a church with which their consciences will not permit them to join." On this basis dissenters of any faith whatever are to be "totally free and exempt from all levies, taxes and impositions," for the support of the church or its ministers.

The third and fourth paragraphs of the law provide for the payment of salaries in arrears to the clergy and guarantee to the church its property-holdings as before the passage of the act. But the fifth and sixth paragraphs have important political implications. In the fifth the question of whether the church is to be supported by a general assessment or by voluntary contributions is deliberately left untouched, indicating a deep division even among the Episcopalians as to the propriety of a tax-supported church. Thus Mason and Madison again maneuvered successfully toward freedom of conscience. They succeeded still further by securing in the sixth and final provision a suspension of the old law for tax support.

In general, the new law had two effects: 1) it positively liberated all dissenters from the influence of the state church, and 2) it paved the way for a thoroughgoing debate on the question whether assessments ought to be levied by law, even on members, for the maintenance of religion. The bill was carried by solid majorities in both houses of the legislature, on what was a kind of wave of liberal sentiment regarding religious questions. The wave carried further, and in 1779 Virginia disestablished the church entirely. But thereafter a reaction set in.

There is no question that the general reaction in favor of state supported religion which took place in the mid-1780's was a part of the whole political and philosophical reaction that followed the Revolution, just as the radical departure from tradition and orthodoxy of 1776-1779 was owing in large part to the revolutionary spirit of that time. What marked off the Republicans from others was their unyielding adherence to the principle of the free conscience. They would alter their political tactics and their demands according to the climate of opinion as they sensed it, but the ultimate purpose was never obscured.

In the Congress, under the Articles of Confederation, there was no proposal of a national church establishment. But in 1785 the Congress did reflect the force of the reaction, when it considered a measure to set aside lands in each district of the western territories for the support

of the religion "of the majority of inhabitants." Madison, writing to
Monroe, speaks scathingly of this proposal, "How a regulation so unjust in itself, so foreign to the authority of Congress, so hurtful to the
sale of the public land, and smelling so strongly of an antiquated bigotry, could have received the countenance of a committee is truly matter of astonishment."[15] The measure died in the committee, and Madison breathed more freely. But in Virginia the move for a general
assessment to support religion was in full stride.

The proposed Virginia bill, which would have levied a general tax
for the support of religious teachers of all Christian denominations,
was postponed on December 24, 1784 for final action one year later. It
was favored by men like Washington, Patrick Henry, Richard Henry
Lee, and John Marshall. Madison led the opposition. In his speech he
took the same ground on which he had argued for full freedom in the
Virginia Declaration. As a major premise he laid it down that "religion
is not within the purview of civil authority."[16] But, recognizing the
temper of the Assembly, he did not press the claims of natural right.
Instead he showed that the civil authority must avoid legislation on religious questions because: a) religion flourishes best when standing on
its own merits, and b) ultimately a state which legislates any sort of
establishment becomes involved in theological controversy, where civil
magistrates have no competence and which subverts the harmony of
society. With regard to the proposed bill itself, Madison singles out the
word "Christian" as modifying "religion," and asks how it is to be defined. He quickly shows that there is serious danger that the state will
find itself in the business of defining orthodoxy and heresy. Thus the
door would be opened for all the old evils. The speech was effective,
but not enough to defeat the bill. He had to be content with a post-
ponement, which gave the advocates of freedom a year of grace to
advance their cause.

By October, 1785, Madison was convinced that the rivalry of sects
was so intense and their relative strength so balanced that to deal with
the religious problem on the radical ground of natural right would now
be politically effective. To this end he drafted his *Memorial and Remonstrance against Religious Assessments,* which together with Jefferson's
bill on religious freedom for which it prepared the way, constitutes the
best articulated and the most profound statement of the American doctrine of the free conscience.

The *Remonstrance* offers fifteen separate objections to "A Bill establishing a Provision for Teachers of the Christian Religion." All are well

considered and appropriate, but the first controls the meaning of the others and marks a genuine turning point in the history of freedom of religion. It is cast in the form of a gloss on the 16th article of the Declaration of Rights, "that Religion . . . can be directed only by reason and conviction, not by force or violence." Madison returns to his own draft of that article and elaborates its central point:

> The Religion then of every man must be left to the conviction and conscience of every man; and it is the right of every man to exercise it as these may dictate. This right is in its nature an unalienable right. It is unalienable; because the opinions of men, depending only on the evidence contemplated by their own minds, cannot follow the dictates of other men: it is unalienable also; because what is here a right towards men, is a duty towards the Creator. It is the duty of every man to render to the Creator such homage, and such only, as he believes to be acceptable to him.[17]

If the freedoms of conscience and worship are natural rights, as Madison here claims, it must follow not only that there can be no justification for an established church—or *religion*—which would *tolerate* others, but that these rights of religion are antecedent and superior to any civil authority formed by social contract. Because religion involves a personal duty of the natural man, natural law will actually prohibit him from surrendering his religious rights to civil society. "We maintain therefore that in matters of Religion, no man's right is abridged by the institution of Civil Society, and that Religion is wholly exempt from its cognizance."[18] This statement is the key to the whole philosophy and explains better, perhaps, than any other the meaning of the First Amendment.

Madison now proceeds to build skillfully on these premises. Thus, if religion is to be exempt from the authority of government in general it surely may not be touched by a legislature. A legislature is itself limited by constitutional provisions for the separation of powers and is directly responsible to its constituents:

> The preservation of a free government requires not merely, that the metes and bounds which separate each department of power may be invariably maintained; but more especially, that neither of them be suffered to overleap the great Barrier which defends the rights of the people.[19]

"Tyrants" may be defined as those who "are guilty of such an encroachment," while those who submit to it are "slaves." Furthermore, "it is proper to take alarm at the first experiment on our liberties." Statements like these are clear warnings of what the Republicans would do about such measures as the Alien and Sedition Acts.

In Madison's time at least ninety-five percent of all American citizens professed Christianity in some form. For this reason it is particularly important to observe that Madison carefully refrained from identifying "the duty which we owe to our Creator" with either Christianity or any other religion. A free government must be secular by definition:

> Who does not see that the same authority which can establish Christianity, in exclusion of all other Religions, may establish with the same ease any particular sect of Christians, in exclusion of all other sects? That the same authority which can force a citizen to contribute three pence only of his property for the support of any one establishment, may force him to conform to any other establishment in all cases whatsoever?[20]

In the twentieth century, when membership in non-Christian religions has reached substantial proportions, the dependence of religious freedom on this position is greater than ever. It is evident, indeed, that under modern conditions Madison would insist upon a clear distinction between secularism in behavior, which is a moral matter, and secularism in government, which is a political matter. The one may properly be the subject of religious exhortations; the other may not. Thus it may be said that a neutral state is the only safeguard for plural values.

In later paragraphs, Madison argues that the bill would violate the principle that all legislation must fall upon citizens equally; that establishment is neither necessary nor desirable for religion to flourish; that civil government does not need the support of a religious establishment (the exact opposite of the Massachusetts declaration); that an establishment of religion—any or all religions—subverts the idea of America as an asylum for the oppressed; that the bill "will have a like tendency to banish our citizens"; that it will disrupt the harmony in which the sects live together, and interfere with the "diffusion of the light of Christianity"; and that because so many are opposed to it, the bill will have a tendency to undermine the authority of all laws.

In conclusion he reverts to the principle that religious freedom is a natural right, in no way derivative from the civil society established by social contract. In this regard the religious right must be recognized as depending upon the same sanction as all other natural rights claimed by the people. If, therefore, government may infringe upon religious freedom, it may with equal justice infringe upon any other:

> Either we must say, that they [the legislature] may control the freedom of the press, may abolish the trial by jury, may swallow up the

Executive and Judiciary powers of the state; nay that they may despoil us of our very right of suffrage, and erect themselves into an independent and hereditary assembly; or we must say, that they have no authority to enact into law the bill under consideration.[21]

No more advanced ground than this could be taken, or has, indeed, ever been attempted. Madison's theory rejected entirely the idea of toleration, rested the freedom of religion upon natural law, and limited the state to exclusively secular functions. What is more remarkable than the radicalism of the position is that, in a society composed almost wholly of Christians accustomed to the state support of their religion, it carried the majority.

Madison's margin of victory in the Assembly was so substantial that he quickly capitalized on his position by introducing and pressing for the adoption of Jefferson's bill for religious freedom. But the strained political situation is suggested by the fact that, in a long letter to Washington, Madison gives a detailed account of the measures before the Assembly and the actions taken without any reference to the assessment bill, which Washington favored, or Jefferson's bill, which Washington might well have opposed. He does mention that the House "have engaged with some alacrity in the consideration of the Revised Code prepared by Mr. Jefferson, Mr. Pendleton, and Mr. Wythe."[22] The code, of course, included the bill for religious freedom, but Madison is careful not to remind Washington of this fact.

Jefferson's bill—for which, together with the Declaration of Independence and the founding of the University of Virginia, he most wished to be remembered—was drawn in 1777 and introduced into the Assembly in 1779. This was the year in which the Episcopal Church was dis-established, and Jefferson meant his bill to replace the old legislation. But his colleagues were not prepared to go so far, and the proposal was tabled. In the session of 1785-1786, under different political conditions, Madison judged that the times were auspicious. He introduced it on October 31. It was considered in committee, debated in the House, and passed back and forth between the House and the Senate for more than two months. But on January 16, 1786, with surprisingly little modification, it became law. On January 22 Madison wrote to Jefferson in Paris, "the enacting clauses past without a single alteration, and I flatter myself have in this country extinguished forever the ambitious hope of making laws for the human mind."[23]

Jefferson's preamble took shape in his mind during the Revolution and proceeded from the same experience and the same meditations as informed the Declaration of Independence. Its doctrine is fully in accord with the assertion of "self-evident" truths, inherent in nature, and discernible by reason. It differs from Madison's *Remonstrance* only in its more positive tone. As the *Remonstrance* was a kind of gloss on the Virginia Declaration of Rights, so it may be said that Jefferson's preamble is a gloss on the Declaration of Independence, helping to explain the meaning of liberty. No paraphrase or piecemeal discussion can substitute for the document itself:

Whereas Almighty God hath created the mind free; that all attempts to influence it by temporal punishments or burthens, or by civil incapacitations, tend only to beget habits of hypocrisy and meanness, and are a departure from the plan of the Holy author of our religion, who being Lord both of body and mind, yet chose not to propagate it by coercions on either, as was in his Almighty power to do; that the impious presumption of legislators and rulers, civil as well as ecclesiastical, who being themselves but fallible and uninspired men, have assumed dominion over the faith of others, setting up their own opinions and modes of thinking as the only true and infallible, and as such endeavoring to impose them on others, hath established and maintained false religions over the greatest part of the world, and through all time; that to compel a man to furnish contributions of money for the propagation of opinions which he disbelieves, is sinful and tyrannical; that even the forcing him to support this or that teacher of his own religious persuasion, is depriving him of the comfortable liberty of giving his contributions to the particular pastor whose morals he would make his pattern, and whose powers he feels most persuasive to righteousness, and is withdrawing from the ministry those temporary rewards, which proceeding from an approbation of their personal conduct, are an additional incitement to earnest and unremitting labours for the instruction of mankind; that our civil rights have no dependence on our religious opinions, any more than our opinions in physics or geometry; that therefore the proscribing any citizen as unworthy the public confidence by laying upon him an incapacity of being called to offices of trust and emolument, unless he profess to renounce this or that religious opinion, is depriving him injuriously of those privileges and advantages to which in common with his fellow-citizens he has a natural right; that it tends only to corrupt the principles of that religion it is meant to encourage, by bribing with a monopoly of worldly honours and emoluments, those who will externally profess and conform to it; that though indeed these are criminal who do not withstand such temptation, yet neither are those innocent who lay the bait in their way; that to suffer the civil magistrate to intrude his powers into the field of opinion, and to restrain the profession or propagation of principles on supposition of their ill tendency, is a dangerous fallacy, which at once destroys all religious liberty, because he being of course judge of that tendency will make his opinions the rule of judgment, and approve or condemn the sentiments of others only as they shall square with or differ from his own; that it is time enough for the rightful purposes of civil government, for its officers to interfere when principles break out into overt acts against peace and good order; and finally, that truth is great and will prevail if left to herself, that she is the proper and sufficient antagonist against error, and has nothing to fear from the conflict, unless by human interposition disarmed of her natural weapons, free argument and debate, errors ceasing to be dangerous when it is permitted freely to contradict them.[24]

The adoption of so full and far-reaching a statement as an integral part of statute law is an indication not only of Madison's political abilities but of the state of mind prevalent in Virginia. Jefferson's bill had been printed in 1779, so that his fellow citizens had had more than six years in which to examine it, debate its merits, and form their opinions. Jefferson himself had been discussing the problem in conversations and correspondence for years, and had dealt with the whole subject in his *Notes on Virginia*, which was written between 1781 and 1783 and published first in 1784. By January of 1786 his views were not only well known in the United States but celebrated in Europe.

Jefferson understood religious freedom, as the bill implies, as an essential part of the all-encompassing freedom of the mind. In the *Notes*, where he had no need to confine himself to the drafting of a particular statute, he makes this point clear. Government, he argues, is disqualified by its nature and function from meddling with matters of opinion, not only in religion but in science and general culture:

Was the government to prescribe to us our medicine and diet, our bodies would be in such keeping as our souls are now [i.e. under an established religion]. Thus in France the emetic was once forbidden as a medicine, the potato as an article of food. Government is just as fallible, too, when it fixes systems in physics. Galileo was sent to the Inquisition for affirming that the earth was a sphere; the government had declared it to be as flat as a trencher, and Galileo was obliged to abjure his error. This error, however, at length prevailed, the earth became a globe, and Descartes declared it was whirled round its axis by a vortex. The government in which he lived was wise enough to see that this was no question of civil jurisdiction, or we should all have been involved by authority in vortices.[25]

In religion, as in all matters of faith and knowledge, reliance must be placed exclusively upon reason and investigation. Freedom advances knowledge; tyranny frustrates it: "It is error alone which needs the support of government. Truth can stand by itself."

While the Virginia Statute of Religious Freedom assumes the validity of religious faith and acknowledges an omnipotent Creator, it exempts all men, unconditionally, from any sort of worship not dependent on their own will. In his *Notes* Jefferson drew the full implication that even atheism is a private matter of which the state can take no cognizance. "The legitimate powers of government extend to such acts only as are injurious to others. But it does me no injury for my neighbor to say there are twenty gods, or no God. It neither picks my pocket nor breaks my leg."[26] On the basis of such statements as this Jefferson was himself frequently denounced as an atheist. The charge, of course, was politically motivated and without foundation. But his view, as expressed in the *Notes*, shows clearly enough that the language of religion in which he cast the Virginia Statute, like that of Madison's *Remonstrance*, was an important part of the political technique which was used to secure its passage.

Jefferson and Madison both saw that a secular government was the first requisite for freedom of the mind. But a statement putting the matter thus baldly would have evoked overwhelming opposition. Wishing to establish freedom of the mind above all else, and believing that freedom would cause religion to flourish, they chose to present the question in terms of a development within the accepted body of tradition and in the accepted world of discourse. The unparalleled, if not untrammeled, freedom of thought which Americans have enjoyed in the ensuing one hundred and seventy years, and the vigorous life of the churches, are ample testimony to the wisdom of their decision and the soundness of their view.

The enacting clauses in Jefferson's bill which, as Madison reported, were passed without alteration, provided in the first, not only that no man should be compelled to "frequent or support any religious worship, place or ministry whatsoever," but also that "all men shall be free to profess, and by argument to maintain, their opinion in matters of religion, and that the same shall in no wise diminish, enlarge or affect their civil capacities." In the second Jefferson reverted to the principle that freedom of religion is a natural right, so that the law enjoins upon future assemblies, which might wish to reverse or repeal the measure, to be mindful that such action would violate natural law. The earth, indeed, belongs to the living, and no legislature may make laws binding on the future, but in enacting this statute it is proper to say that no legislature can justly overset what is established by nature.

One further note may be added here to display Madison's adroit strategy. In June, 1784 the Assembly considered and passed a measure to incorporate the Episcopal Church. The bill recognized the church as a body politic and authorized the clergy and the vestrymen in annual convention to act on behalf of the church in all matters pertaining to ritual, doctrine, and church practice, as well as to serve as proprietors of all church property. The bill had substantial merit as clarifying certain questions which arose by reason of the separation from England and the dis-establishment. Madison saw these advantages, but thought them less consequential than the implied principle that a legislature could make laws regarding religion. However, he voted for the bill on the ground that to oppose it would weaken his position on the question of a general assessment by alienating the large bloc of Episcopalians in the Assembly. But two years later, after the assessment had been defeated and the Statute of Religious Freedom enacted, he pressed the advantage still further and drafted a petition, for submission by others, against the incorporation statute. The central objection Madison offered was that "the law admits the power of the Legislature to interfere in matters of Religion which we think is not included in their jurisdiction."[27] It was finally repealed in January, 1787. Thus, instead of precipitating a bitter controversy over a secondary matter, he waited patiently until it could be used as a test case under the general statute. The strategy worked perfectly and both purposes were achieved. Thereafter it would be a rash business to ask a Virginia legislature to meddle in religious affairs, or otherwise entertain "the ambitious hope of making laws for the human mind."

III

In the Constitutional Convention of 1787 there was tacit agreement to avoid the religious question so far as possible. Madison, engrossed in the consummate political task of forming a republican government in balance between national and state authority, seems to have thought it inexpedient to press his colleagues on the question of religion. The two principal measures regarding religious freedom were offered by Charles Pinckney of South Carolina. The first—"The legislature of the United States shall pass no law on the subject of religion"—was not adopted, on the ground that enumeration of the powers of the various branches was sufficient protection. The second—forbidding religious tests for officeholding—eventually formed the final clause of Article VI.[28]

Madison records the original language of Pinckney's second proposal as follows: "No religious test or qualification shall ever be annexed to any oath of office under the authority of the United States." The debate following the proposal dealt almost exclusively with a question as to the most appropriate place to include it. Roger Sherman of Connecticut did express the view that it was an unnecessary provision—"the prevailing liberality being a sufficient security against such tests." But two men who later became leading Federalists, Gouverneur Morris and General Charles C. Pinckney, saved Madison the trouble of arguing the matter by supporting the measure strongly. Ultimately the clause was annexed to the article providing for an oath of office for both state and federal officials. But the national government only was forbidden to ask questions bearing on religion, out of deference to states where established churches still prevailed. The adopted language contained no significant alteration of Pinckney's intent: "no religious Test shall ever be required as a Qualification to any office or public trust under the United States."[29]

If Madison's reticence at the Convention on the question of freedom of conscience seems somewhat curious in the light of his remarkable political campaign in Virginia, it must be remembered that he took a similar attitude toward the whole problem of a bill of rights. As we saw in Chapter II, he was prepared to adopt a Constitution without a bill of rights for two leading reasons: the intrinsic difficulty of securing agreement to specific provisions, and the principle that it was sufficient to enumerate the powers of the national government and reserve all other powers to the states or to the people. In presenting the matter to Jefferson he called attention to the fortunate balance of power as among the religious denominations in Virginia which had permitted passage of the bill for religious freedom. The case was different in the Convention, where he had to deal with a number of powerful states in which churches were established. Better, he thought, to leave the matter untouched than to precipitate a bitter debate which might jeopardize the adoption of any republican constitution. If a popular demand for a bill of rights, with a provision for religious freedom, should develop later, an appropriate amendment could be enacted without such risks.

An emphatic demand for a bill of rights did, of course, arise, not only from individuals like Jefferson, but from most of the state ratifying conventions. This demand gave Madison the opportunity he sought when the first Congress assembled. In his speech to the House on June 8, 1789 he offered an amendment which would enact the full intent of the Virginia principle and would make it binding not only on the national government but on the states as well:

> The civil rights of none shall be abridged on account of religious belief or worship, nor shall any national religion be established, nor shall the full and equal rights of conscience be in any manner, or on any pretext, infringed.
> No State shall violate the equal rights of conscience, or the freedom of the press, or the trial by jury in criminal cases.

The debate began on August 15. Madison defended his proposal as follows:

> Mr. Madison said, he apprehended the meaning of the words to be, that Congress should not establish a religion, and enforce the legal observation of it by law, nor compel men to worship God in any manner contrary to their conscience. Whether the words are necessary or not, he did not mean to say, but they had been required by some of the State Conventions, who seemed to entertain an opinion that under the clause of the constitution, which gave power to Congress to make all laws necessary and proper to carry into execution the constitution, and the laws made under it, enabled them to make laws of such nature as might infringe the rights of conscience, and establish a national religion; to prevent these effects he presumed the amendment was intended, and he thought it as well expressed as the nature of the language would admit.

and further, as to prohibition against the states:

> Mr. Madison conceived this to be the most valuable amendment in the whole list. If there was any reason to restrain the Government of the United States from infringing upon these essential rights, it was equally necessary that they should be secured against the State Governments. He thought that if they provided against the one, it was as necessary to provide against the other, and was satisfied that it would be equally grateful to the people.[30]

In the ensuing weeks the language of the proposed amendment was altered many times, both in the House and in the Senate. The clause affecting the powers of the states was finally dropped entirely because of pressure from the states in which religion was established. But the language of the first portion was improved and sharpened to Madison's full satisfaction. House and Senate finally concurred on September 25—"Congress shall make no law respecting an establishment of religion, or prohibiting the free exercise thereof."[31] Ultimately, of course, through a long series of court cases, both before and after adoption of the Fourteenth Amendment, the restriction and prohibition thus enacted became binding upon the states.[32]

As we have said, and as the record shows, neither the development of the philosophy of the free conscience, its statutory enactment in Virginia, nor its inclusion in the Constitution of the United States may be called an exclusive achievement of the Republican Party. But there can be no question that Jefferson and Madison made decisive contributions in the realm of ideas and that Mason and, especially, Madison exercised political leadership of the highest order, a leadership without which there might well have been a very long delay before full religious freedom could be realized. It is equally certain that, in the first decades after the Constitution went into effect, the Republican Party took up the doctrine of Madison and Jefferson and employed it as a fixed standard for evaluating any and every measure which might infringe upon human freedom.

IV

Republican solicitude for religious freedom, as protected by an absolute separation of church and state, runs like a theme through the political and legislative controversies of the 1790's. This is not to suggest that Federalist administrations or Federalist-controlled Congresses ever proposed to infringe on the liberty of conscience as such. But the Republicans were quick to see the possibilities of such infringements in typical Federalist measures which rested on implied powers in the Constitution.

Madison very early served notice as to what his attitude would be, and in connection with a bill offered by himself. On January 25, 1790 he introduced a bill to provide for a federal census based on an enumeration of citizens according to occupations. He included the fields of agriculture, commerce, and industry but omitted the professions. When he was asked on the floor of the House why he had not included them he replied:

> As to those who are employed in teaching and inculcating the duties of religion, there may be some indelicacy in singling them out, as the general government is proscribed from interfering, in any manner whatever, in matters respecting religion; and it may be thought to do this, in ascertaining who [are], and who are not ministers of the gospel.[33]

Thus it was not surprising that Madison, and other Republicans, should attack Hamilton's bill for a United States Bank on the ground that it implied powers in the national government which could be extended into the fields of religion and of opinion generally. As we have already seen, Madison thought that the power to incorporate a bank, unless specifically granted by the Constitution—which it was not—would imply a power to incorporate religion. The matter is worth reviewing in the present context. In his speech of February 2, 1791 Madison spoke particularly of the point made in defense of the bank bill, that it did not interfere with the rights of the states:

> If Congress could incorporate a Bank merely because the act would leave the States free to establish Banks also, any other incorporations might be made by Congress. They could incorporate companies of manufacturers, or companies for cutting canals, or even religious societies, leaving similar incorporations by the States, like State Banks, to themselves. Congress might even establish religious teachers in every parish, and pay them out of the Treasury of the United States, leaving other teachers unmolested in their functions.

Again, reverting to the argument which had been adduced to show that a bill of rights was unnecessary because powers not enumerated were reserved, Madison pointed out that "on any other supposition, the power of Congress to abridge the freedom of the press, or the rights of conscience, etc., could not have been disproved."[34] The Federalists did not, of course, draw such an implication from their victory on the question of the bank. But it is significant that they studiously ignored Madison's contention, preferring to defend the bank wholly in terms of economic expediency lest a majority, persuaded of a threat to religious freedom, be rallied against them.

One further illustration of the Republican position will suffice. In the bitter struggle over the Sedition Act the Republicans made a central point of the danger to freedom of the mind and conscience. The Address of 1799 from the Assembly to the people of Virginia, drafted by Madison, deals twice—emphatically—with the Sedition Act as an unconstitutional violation of religious freedom. The Act implied that a distinction between liberty and licentiousness could properly be applied by the executive branch of the government in asking for indictments for the expression of seditious opinions. Madison denounced this assumed power as an evident encroachment on individual freedom, and related it directly to religion:

> Under it men of a particular religious opinion might be excluded from office, because such exclusion would not amount to an establishment of religion, and because it might be said that their opinions are licentious. And under it Congress might denominate a religion to be heretical and licentious, and proceed to its suppression.

It would be well, Madison added, to remember that "it is to the press mankind are indebted for having dispelled the clouds which long encompassed religion, for disclosing her genuine lustre, and disseminating her salutary doctrines."[35]

Later on, as we saw in Chapter II, the Address deals again with the freedom of the mind, as illustrated by freedom of religious opinions. The passage is worth repeating:

> The sacred obligations of religion flow from the due exercise of opinion, in the solemn discharge of which man is accountable to his God alone; yet, under this precedent the truth of religion itself may be ascertained, and its pretended licentiousness punished by a jury of a different creed from that held by the person accused. This law, then, commits the double sacrilege of arresting reason in her progress towards perfection, and of placing in a state of danger the free exercise of religious opinions.

Thus there is a "higher law" than the Constitution, and which is acknowledged by the First Amendment. As Madison had argued in his *Remonstrance*, the freedom of opinion and the freedom of worship are inalienable rights of the natural man. They neither are nor can be surrendered by his entrance into civil society. This was the meaning of the Virginia Statute and of the First Amendment. Natural law requires an absolute separation of church from state, of government from religion.

It could be argued against Madison that he had condoned the hiring of chaplains for the Congress of the United States and for the armed forces, a practice which constituted a kind of establishment. He was sensitive to this point, but since it was a tradition inherited from the old Congress and had been initiated as a measure for national unity during the Revolution, he thought it expedient to allow sentiment this minor triumph at the expense of principle. On the other hand, where precedents were to be established, as in the Bank bill or the Sedition Act, he was convinced that it would be fatal to yield an inch.

V

When the Sedition Act lapsed, coincident with the coming of the Republicans to power in March, 1801, it became a certainty that the First Amendment would continue to be interpreted as expressing the doctrine of the unalienable freedom of conscience. In the Presidency, both Jefferson and Madison improved upon every opportunity to establish significant precedents either by public pronouncement or by official action.

The most famous of such pronouncements was, of course, Jefferson's message to the Danbury, Connecticut Baptist Association on January 1, 1802. Acknowledging a letter of greeting to the President, containing an expression of appreciation for his liberal attitude in religious matters, Jefferson took the occasion to make a definitive statement of the American principle:

> Believing with you that religion is a matter which lies solely between man and his God, that he owes account to none other for his faith or his worship, that the legislative powers of government reach actions only, and not opinions, I contemplate with sovereign reverence that act of the whole American people which declared that their legislature should "make no law respecting an establishment of religion, or prohibiting the free exercise thereof," thus building a wall of separation between Church and State. Adhering to this expression of the supreme will of the nation in behalf of the rights of conscience, I shall see with sincere satisfaction the progress of those sentiments which tend to restore to man all his natural rights, convinced he has no natural right in opposition to his social duties.[36]

If there is here an echo of George Mason's 1775 speech at Fairfax—"to restore mankind to its native rights"—it is not accidental. The "wall of separation between Church and State" is only a logical application of the whole philosophy of natural law and natural right which never ceased to guide Republican thinking. It is a wall built by the consensus of free men. Its materials are ideas and judicial findings, and unlike physical structures it improves with age. There have always been some Americans who would wish to tear it down. There are such in the present day. There are even those who doubt its existence. But when the Supreme Court denies the right of the Board of Regents of New York State to ban a motion picture because some citizens think it sacrilegious, it is clear that the ancient wall is firmly standing.

A veto message by Madison may serve as an example of the manner in which the Republicans used the Presidency to enforce the First Amendment. In 1811 Madison received a bill from Congress providing for a grant of land to the Baptist Church of Salem, Mississippi. His veto was quick and sure:

> Because the bill in reserving a certain parcel of land of the United States for the use of said Baptist Church comprises a principle and precedent for the appropriation of funds of the United States for the use and support of religious societies, contrary to the article of the Constitution which declares that "Congress, shall make no law respecting a religious establishment."[37]

The present day student of the problem will have no difficulty in recognizing here a classic precedent for such an opinion as that of Mr. Justice Black in *Everson v. Board of Education*: "No tax in any amount, large or small, can be levied to support any religious activities or institutions, whatever they may be called, or whatever form they may adopt to teach or practise religion."[38]

Jefferson, Madison, and other Republicans looked upon the sixth article of the Constitution and the First Amendment as together establishing a code of behavior for government. Their enforcement was vigorous and their leadership spirited. It was not simply a coincidence that the last state churches were abolished during the Republican ascendancy. But they were not satisfied to rest the freedom of the mind upon statutes and courts. As in all other matters, the citizens themselves would ultimately determine the efficacy of liberty. Writing to Dr. Rush in 1803, Jefferson speaks in deeply serious terms of the role of the individual citizen:

> I am moreover averse to the communication of my religious tenets to the public; because it would countenance the presumption of those who have endeavored to draw them before that tribunal, and to seduce public opinion to erect itself into that inquisition over the rights of conscience, which the laws have so justly proscribed. It behooves every man who values liberty of conscience for himself, to resist invasions of it in the case of others; or their case may, by change of

circumstances, become his own. It behooves him, too, in his own case, to give no example of concession, betraying the common right of independent opinion, by answering questions of faith, which the laws have left between God and himself.[39]

If Jefferson were to survey the scene in the mid-twentieth century he might well be reassured by the splendid defense of religious freedom he would find in the Supreme Court, but he would certainly be disheartened, if not appalled, at the spectacle of a public servant testifying on his religious beliefs before a Senate Investigating Committee.[40]

In the closing days of his administration, Jefferson received innumerable messages and formal addresses from state legislatures and from groups of private citizens expressing appreciation of his character and his government. His carefully composed replies, taken together, make a sort of summary of his philosophy and his political program. Through them all runs pride in his support of the free conscience. One passage is particularly worthy of notice. He used it several times, and it may safely be considered a representative statement of the Republican view:

> ... a recollection of our former vassalage in religion and civil government, will unite the zeal of every heart, and the energy of every hand, to preserve that independence in both which, under the favor of heaven, a disinterested devotion to the public cause first achieved, and a disinterested sacrifice of private interests will now maintain.[41]

NOTES

1. Anson Phelps Stokes's *Church and State in the United States*, 3 vols., 1950, is a monumental work treating every phase of the problem in detail and including all relevant documents.
2. Stuart Gerry Brown, ed., *We Hold These Truths*, 2d ed. 1948, 53.
3. *Ibid.*
4. John Locke, *A Letter Concerning Toleration*, (ed. C. L. Sherman, 1937), 183.
5. The contention of liberal historians, like Vernon Parrington, that Roger Williams was the "father of religious freedom" is well intentioned but seriously inaccurate. The uniquely American theory of the secular or neutral state presupposes an ultimate value in freedom itself which was at the furthest remove from Williams's thinking. See Perry Miller's *Roger Williams* (1953) for a definitive analysis of this question.
6. Brant, *Madison*, I, 244. Brant's discussion here (241-250) gives the most authoritative account of the development of Article 16, particularly in regard to the roles played by Mason and Madison. Stokes, though he benefits from Brant's researches, is less satisfactory.
7. Madison, *Writings*, I, 19, (24 January, 1774).

8. *Ibid.*, 21.
9. Brant, *op. cit.*, 245.
10. Thomas Paine, *Representative Selections*, ed. H. H. Clark, 106.
11. Brant, *op. cit.*, 246.
12. *Ibid.*, 247.
13. Brown, *We Hold These Truths*, 36.
14. The text here cited is given in Stokes, *Church and State in the United States*, I, 304-305.
15. Madison, *Writings*, II, 145, (29 May, 1785).
16. *Ibid.*, 88. Only Madison's notes and outline of the speech survive.
17. *Ibid.*, 184.
18. *Ibid.*, 185.
19. *Ibid.*
20. *Ibid.*, 186.
21. *Ibid.*, 191.
22. *Ibid.*, 191 ff. (11 November, 1785).
23. *Ibid.*, 216. A careful account of the changes in the bill and a full history of its passage are given in *The Papers of Thomas Jefferson*, II, 547-553.
24. Brown, *We Hold These Truths*, 36-37. A composite text showing changes made during passage of the bill is given in *The Papers of Thomas Jefferson*, II, 545-546.
25. Jefferson, *Writings*, III, 264.
26. *Ibid.*, 263.
27. Madison, *Writings*, II, 213. Ultimately, Madison's view on this point was over-ruled by the Supreme Court. See *Terrett v. Taylor*, 9 Cranch 43, 49 (U.S. 1815).
28. Stokes excerpts the passages relevant to the religious problem from Madison's *Notes*, in *Church and State in the United States*, I, 526 ff.
29. Brown, *We Hold These Truths*, 87.
30. *Annals of Congress*, 15, 17 August, 1789.
31. Brant, *Madison*, III, 268-271, argues convincingly that the amendment as adopted was written by Madison, but Stokes gives substantial credit to Liver-more and Ames.
32. Stokes, *Church and State in the United States*, I, 565-599, gives a detailed history of these cases.
33. *Annals of Congress*, 25 January, 1790.
34. Madison, *Writings*, VI, 28-29, 34.
35. *Ibid.*, 335-336.
36. Jefferson, *Works*, ed. Washington, VIII, 113.
37. Cited by Brant, *Madison*, III, 272. See also Madison's letter to North Carolina Baptists, 3 June, 1811, (*Congress Edition*, II, 511-512).
38. Stokes, *Church and State in the United States*, I, 592. (330 U.S. 1, 16, 1947.)
39. Jefferson, *Works*, ed. Washington, IV, 480, (21 April, 1803).
40. See the *New York Times*, 3 March, 1953, for the investigation by the McCar-thy Committee of Roger Lyons.
41. Jefferson, *Works*, ed. Washington, VIII, 138.

We shall have our follies without doubt. Some one or more of them will always be afloat. But ours will be the follies of enthusiasm, not of bigotry, not of Jesuitism. Bigotry is the disease of ignorance, or morbid minds; enthusiasm of the free and buoyant. Education and free discussion are the antidotes of both. We are destined to be a barrier against the returns of ignorance and barbarism. Old Europe will have to lean on our shoulders, and to hobble along by our side, under the monkish trammels of priests and kings, as she can. What a colossus shall we be when the southern continent comes up to our mark! What a stand will it secure as a ralliance for the reason and freedom of the globe! I like the dreams of the future better than the history of the past.

— Thomas Jefferson, 1816.

CHAPTER SIX

Conclusion

JEFFERSON, from the privacy of his retirement, rhetorically asked John Adams, "but whither is senile garrulity leading me? Into politics, of which I have taken final leave. I think little of them and say less. I have given up newspapers in exchange for Tacitus and Thucydides, for Newton and Euclid, and I find myself much the happier."[1] Though he is guilty of a measure of exaggeration, Jefferson's statement is substantially true. And he speaks in the deepest spirit of the Republican movement. Jefferson, Madison, Monroe, and Gallatin, maintained a quick interest and a significant influence on public life throughout their long years, but politics was never more than a means, either for them or for their associates. The great burden of Republicanism was the securing of individual liberty, and the end was the good life. The dearest of men's possessions was the property of privacy, politics the means to obtain it.

Adherence to freedom—freedom of action and of thought, freedom from all oppression, whether by government or by society—drew together the republicans of the early United States and made them a party with a positive program, while the Federalist reaction, as they saw it, guided the direction and scope of their attack. But devotion to science, agriculture, the arts, and philosophy provided them with a still firmer bond of union. It was no accident that in the midst of a bitter political struggle Madison could interrupt a letter to Jefferson to give an account of the meteorological phenomena he was recording at Montpelier, or that Monroe found time at the very height of the party battles to dream with Madison of a life without slavery on their rolling acres in central New York, or that Gallatin never wrote to his wife from the sessions of Congress without bitter regrets that the public business kept him from his beloved Pennsylvania hills.

161

Thus it was that plans for public education were always central in Republican thought. On the one hand, the blessings of liberty could not be enjoyed unless the citizens were educated, so far as their capabilities would permit, to cherish and use it wisely; while, on the other, liberty itself could be achieved and maintained only by a people of cultivated and responsible understanding. As Monroe put it, "It is an opinion which I have long entertained, and which every day's experience and observation tends to confirm, that however free our political institutions may be in the commencement, liberty cannot long be preserved unless the society in every district, in all its members, possesses that portion of useful knowledge which is necessary to qualify them to discharge with credit and effect, those great duties of citizens on which free Government rests." And further, "the responsibility of public servants, however well provided for by the Constitution, becomes vain and useless if the people in general are not competent judges, in the course of the administration, of all the questions which it involves."[2]

The Republicans were almost congenitally sceptical of proposals for governmental action where affairs could be handled by private citizens. The federal government was to be kept out of the business of the states so far as possible, and the states were to be kept out of the business of private citizens so far as possible. The great plan of internal improvements—the most comprehensive proposal for positive governmental action offered during the whole early history of the United States— was no exception. Its purpose was to facilitate the growth and prosperity of private agriculture, commerce, and industry, and it was to be carried out in all respects, save planning and finance, by the states and local government. But education was a different matter. The republican experiment in America was dependent upon it, and so it was a necessary governmental and public concern. The states should assume the responsibility for the general education of their citizens at whatever public expense might be necessary. It would be appropriate for the national government itself to establish and maintain a university in which the highest education and scholarship of the country might be centralized.

The basis of the Republican position on public education was established in three bills drawn by Jefferson during the revisal of the Virginia code in 1778. The first, "A Bill for the More General Diffusion of Knowledge," commenced with a typical Jeffersonian preamble which remains the classic statement of the relation between education and free government; the second proposed to convert the College of William and Mary into something like a state university; the third, "A Bill for

Establishing a Public Library," provided for a centrally situated public repository of books and other materials for the use of scholars.[3] Jefferson hoped that a system such as these bills embodied would be adopted by all the states. As President he repeatedly asked the Congress, as did Madison, to establish a national university which would round out the educational program for the whole country. It is fair to observe that his plan remained the most comprehensive and best articulated until the appearance of the *Report of the President's Commission on Higher Education* in 1946. But it received only fragmentary realization during Jefferson's lifetime, and the idea of a federal university has never been taken very seriously in the United States.

The first of Jefferson's three bills contains detailed specifications for the distribution and financing of public schools and the selection of pupils for promotion and education at public expense. In certain respects the bill is suggestive of the typical pattern of state education which actually evolved in Virginia and most of the other American states. But the enduring value of the whole scheme lies in the principles it proposes to implement. Its author, writing to Wythe from Paris in 1786, said without reservation that "by far the most important bill in our whole code, is that for the diffusion of knowledge among the people."[4] There is "no other sure foundation . . . for the preservation of freedom and happiness."

The preamble sets forth three leading ideas, 1) that public enlightenment is the only ultimate security against tyranny; 2) that wise and honest laws require wise and honest lawmakers who have the benefit of liberal education; and 3) that since wise and honest men frequently have inadequate financial backing, the most promising children of poor families should be educated at public expense. As for the first, Jefferson argues that even under the most skillfully devised forms of government, "those entrusted with power have, in time, and by slow operations, perverted it into tyranny." The means to prevent such a development in America will be "to illuminate, as far as practicable, the minds of the people at large, and more especially to give them knowledge of those facts, which history exhibiteth, that, possessed thereby of the experience of other ages and countries, they may be enabled to know ambition under all its shapes, and prompt to exert their natural powers to defeat its purposes." The common schools are charged with meeting this need. While their curriculum shall remain, according to tradition and practical utility, mainly reading, writing and arithmetic, education toward awareness of the meaning of tyranny and the corrupting quality of power is to proceed at the same time, because "the books which shall be used . . . for instructing the children to read shall be such as will . . . make them acquainted with Grecian, Roman, English, and American history."[5]

The second and third points in the preamble involve Jefferson's theory of an aristocracy of "virtue and talents" as opposed to an aristocracy of birth and wealth. In this respect the bill is to be understood as a part of a unified system, which includes Jefferson's bills against entail and primogeniture and his proposal to broaden the suffrage by distribution of public land so that all adult males could meet the property qualification. The bill for religious freedom would put all citizens on the basis of equality in the realm of the spirit. The point of the whole was to prevent the inheritance of dominant status either by reason of wealth or legalized privilege, and to encourage the ascent to leadership of the wisest and most virtuous citizens. Universal free primary education would produce a body of citizens capable of understanding and supporting the institutions of liberty. Providing free secondary and higher education for poor boys who proved their merit in standardized competition would reduce the importance of economic advantage as a factor in the emergence of leaders.

In this way Jefferson anticipated the development of an elite of "virtue and talent" which would earn its power by personal achievement and would govern by general consent. This is to envision neither a society of stratified classes nor a society of pure equality. It is, rather, to conceive of free society as based upon the principle of equality of opportunity, allowing each man to find his proper level and function, and hence his happiness. Thus free society is fluid. Absolutes are intolerable. As we saw at the outset, the republican philosophy rejected equally the natural depravity of Hobbes and the natural benevolence of Rousseau. Instead it proposed to foster the best possible development of human potentiality without expecting either too much or too little. Herein lay the essential differences which separated the Republicans from both the Jacobins of the French Revolution and the American Federalists.

In this perspective, according to Jefferson's plan, the grammar or secondary schools would proceed to the central studies of liberal education. The Latin and Greek languages, English grammar and rhetoric, would cultivate the mind and prepare it for the studies which heighten the imagination—literature and philosophy; while geography and advanced arithmetic would prepare the way for scientific understanding.[6]

The tuition in these schools would be moderate, so that many children could be educated at their parents' expense, but the more promising of the poor would continue at public expense.

The university, again open to those who could afford it and to others through competitive scholarships, would be devoted to all the useful sciences.[7] The aim of the university would be to graduate men liberated from ignorance, error, and prejudice and humanized by the understanding of human experience as recorded in history and literature. At the same time these graduates would, through their introduction to science, understand the meaning of change and the possibilities of a better life. They would be prepared to assume places of leadership in society and to make creative contributions to its culture. Such status as they achieved would be the reward of merit, hence less subject to insidious envy and malice. And they could be trusted to cherish and perfect the liberty of the people. They provided the only practical alternative to an established governing class. "If anybody thinks," Jefferson wrote to Wythe from Paris, "that kings, nobles, or priests are good conservators of the public happiness, send him here. It is the best school in the universe to cure him of his folly." He continues in a well-known passage which is worth repeating:

> He will see here, with his own eyes, that these descriptions of men are an abandoned confederacy against the happiness of the mass of the people. The omnipotence of their effect cannot be better proved, than in this country particularly, where, notwithstanding the finest soil upon earth, the finest climate under heaven, and a people of the most benevolent, the most gay and amiable character of which the human form is susceptible; where such a people, I say, surrounded by so many blessings from nature, are loaded with misery, by kings, nobles, and priests, and by them alone. Preach, my dear Sir, a crusade against ignorance; establish and improve the law for educating the common people. Let our countrymen know, that the people alone can protect us against these evils, and that the tax which will be paid for this purpose, is not more than the thousandth part of what will be paid to kings, priests and nobles, who will rise up among us if we leave the people in ignorance.[8]

This whole conception of a body of enlightened citizens, producing, through equal opportunity, its own elite of merit lies at the heart of Republicanism taken at its best, just as John Adams's conception of an aristocracy of "the rich, the beautiful, and well-born" lies at the heart of Federalism taken at its best.

II

When, in 1811, Benjamin Rush undertook to bring about a renewal of the long interrupted friendship between Jefferson and John Adams, he became a principal benefactor of American culture. For the correspondence between the two aging revolutionists is one of the finest specimens of American literature. The tone of the letters is scholarly and speculative, and they are filled with a warmth of understanding and affection. Patriotism, learning, shared experience, and a sense for spiritual adventure brought Jefferson and Adams into a common world of discourse. They had common roots in the Enlightenment, and in their old age, when the republic they had helped to found had moved into a new and sharply different phase of its history, they discovered a closer and deeper affinity than they had known before. But the warmth of friendship and the harmony of opinion may easily be misconceived. The bitter political quarrels of their days of responsibility are all but forgotten; each is anxious to represent himself to the other in the most favorable light. The differences remaining are philosophical only and urbanely moderated, but they are crucial. Their discussion of aristocracy is literary and speculative, but beneath it lie precisely the opposing views of man and of society which always divided the Republicans and the Federalists. As Jefferson put it (and Adams agreed), "whig and tory belong to natural history."

Adams opened the subject by recalling how he and Jefferson had differed as to the prospects of the French Revolution. "When Lafayette harangued you, and me, and John Quincy Adams, through a whole evening, in your hotel in the *Cul de Sac*, at Paris, and developed the plans now in operation to reform France, though I was silent as you was, I then thought I could say something new to him. In plain truth, I was astonished at the grossness of his ignorance of government and history, as I had been for years before at that of Turgot, Rochefoucauld, Condorcet, and Franklin."[9] He recalls that the latter had suggested to him, in this connection, that he write something on aristocracy, and that he did so in his *Defence of the Constitutions* . . . and *Discourses on Davila*. These, he says, "were the cause of that immense unpopularity which fell like the tower of Siloam upon me. Your steady defence of democratical principles, and your invariable favorable opinion of the French Revolution, laid the foundation of your unbounded popularity. *Sic transit gloria mundi*."[10]

The position Adams took in his two controversial books, and re-stated in the ensuing series of letters to Jefferson, is classical and conservative. It assumes that there is a natural inequality among men and that the great majority will convert liberty into license whenever opportunity presents itself. "I have never read reasoning more absurd . . . than the subtle labors of Helvetius and Rousseau to demonstrate the natural equality of mankind. *Jus cuique*, the golden rule, do as you would be done by, is all the equality that can be supported or defended by reason or common sense."[11] It followed that any form of government, whether monarchic, oligarchic, or republican, would depend for the maintenance of order upon an aristocratic class whose status was fixed and unquestioned. Popular admiration and respect for good birth and wealth suggested the principal criteria for such a class. Further, history showed that beauty and talent were most frequently found among the aristocrats of birth and wealth.

> Now, my friend, who are the *aristoi*? Philosophers may answer, 'the wise and good.' But the world, mankind, have, by their practice, always answered, 'the rich, the beautiful, and well-born.' And philosophers themselves, in marrying their children, prefer the rich, the handsome, and the well-descended, to the wise and good.[12]

He proceeds to lay it down that the "five pillars of aristocracy are beauty, wealth, birth, genius, and virtue," and that "any one of the three first can, at any time, overbear any of or both of the two last." You may "call this principle, prejudice, folly, ignorance, baseness, slavery, stupidity, adulation, superstition, or what you will, I will not contradict you. But the fact in natural, moral, political, and domestic history, I will not deny, or dispute, or question."

On such premises democracy in its pure form is not only utopian, but inherently dangerous to personal liberty, as Aristotle long ago demonstrated. Even a democratic republic, for all its careful constitutional restrictions on immediate popular control, does not obviate the difficulty. This was why Adams had predicted to Jefferson that the French Revolution would end in tyranny. His view is strikingly similar to Burke's:

> You was well persuaded in your own mind that the nation would succeed in establishing a free republican government. I was well persuaded in mine, that a project of such a government, over five-and-twenty millions of people, when four-and-twenty millions and five hundred thousand of them could neither read nor write, was as unnatural, irrational, and impracticable as it would be over the elephants,

lions, tigers, panthers, wolves, and bears, in the royal menagerie at Versailles. Napoleon has lately invented a word, which perfectly expressed my opinion at that time and ever since. He calls the project *ideology*; and John Randolph, though he was, fourteen years ago, as wild an enthusiast for equality and fraternity as any of them, appears to be now a regenerated proselyte to Napoleon's opinion and mine, that it was all madness.[13]

Jefferson might well have defended himself against the implication that he had been a visionary in regard to the French Revolution. Actually he had been a moderating influence upon his friends Lafayette, Condorcet, and Rochefoucauld. When they hoped for immediate destruction of the monarchy and the quick creation of a free republic, he had advised caution and tried to show them how a carefully developed constitution could at once preserve the cohesive principles represented by the monarchy and liberalize the laws toward freedom for the people.[14] His opinions of the French situation, as he watched it develop in its early stages, display Jefferson's political acumen at its best. He was no doctrinaire and no "ideologist." He fully appreciated the difference between the attempt to establish a free republic with a highly literate body of citizens already schooled to the responsibilities of liberty, and the hope of building such a republic upon the ashes of a despotism overthrown by violence. John Randolph, whose defection from Republicanism Adams so thoroughly enjoyed, was of a different sort. His early services to the Republican Party were substantial, but he was mercurial in his views and tempestuous in his character. Neither Jefferson nor the other Republican leaders ever gave him their full confidence.

But Jefferson said none of these things to Adams. He was content to ignore the ironic thrusts in favor of a restatement of the fundamental conception of Republicanism, this time in the form of a theory of "natural aristocracy." Into the pages of a single letter he distilled the spirit of the Republican philosophy which his educational system was intended to nourish and maintain. Jefferson manages with appealing literary skill a transition from apparent agreement with Adams to fundamental difference. "I agree with you that there is a natural aristocracy among men," he writes. "The grounds of this are virtue and talents. Formerly, bodily powers gave place among the aristoi. But since the invention of gunpowder has armed the weak as well as the strong with missile death, bodily strength, like beauty, good humor, politeness and other accomplishments, has become but an auxiliary ground of distinction."[15] The next sentence, which evoked no response from Adams, is the classic riposte of the "natural whig" to the "natural tory." *"There is also an artificial aristocracy, founded on wealth and birth, without either virtue or talents; for with these it would belong to the first class."*[16] Thus the qualities to which Adams gave the preponderant importance in defining aristocracy are taken by the Republican as "auxiliary" and "artificial" only. Freedom and equality demand that they be diminished, not privileged. "May we not even say, that that form of government is best, which provides the most effectually for a pure selection of these natural aristoi into the offices of government? The artificial aristocracy is a mischievous ingredient in government, and provision should be made to prevent its ascendancy."[17] From the Bill of Rights to the plan of internal improvements the Republican Party was consistently guided by this conviction.

Next Jefferson turns his attention to Adams's argument from history, that the aristocracy of birth and wealth must take political precedence if anarchy and corruption are to be avoided. This view, Jefferson thought, grew out of a false analogy between the old world and the new. "With respect to aristocracy, we should further consider, that before the establishment of the American States, nothing was known to history but the man of the old world, crowded within limits either small or overcharged, and steeped in the vices which that situation generates. A government adapted to such men would be one thing; but a very different one, that for the man of these States."[18] In America no one is crowded or oppressed. There is land enough for every man who wishes it, and opportunity for any man who wishes to live by industry. The American, by means of his own free labor, may have not only a prosperous working life but a secure old age. Such men have a stake in the maintenance of social order. "Every one, by his property, or by his satisfactory situation, is interested in the support of law and order. And such men may safely and advantageously reserve to themselves a wholesome control over their public affairs, and a degree of freedom, which, in the hands of the *canaille* of the cities of Europe, would be instantly perverted to the demolition and destruction of everything public and private."[19] The true lesson of history, therefore, is not an analogy between the European past and the American future, but the contrast. It is the difference in the condition of men which has made a failure of liberty in Europe and secured the status of the "artificial aristocracy," while in America the artificial have given place to the natural aristoi and liberty has prevailed—difference in the *condition*, not the *nature* of men.

Finally, Jefferson counters Adams's studied pejorism with an equally studied meliorism. There is no dispute as to the failure of the French Revolution. Whigs and tories, Federalists and Republicans can at least agree in their abhorrence of terror. But to see in the revolutionary ferment of Europe nothing more than fresh confirmation of the ancient prejudice against democracy and the power of men to govern themselves in freedom, is to miss the meaning of the whole modern movement—"even in Europe a change has sensibly taken place in the mind of man." The change is occurring at two levels and has two different causes. At the level of "those who read and reflect," it is the scientific revolution—the radically new insights of Bacon and Newton—which is freeing ideas from their old rigid molds. At the level of "the people," it is the American Revolution which sets an example and renews the hope of liberty. "An insurrection has consequently begun, of science, talents, and courage, against rank and birth, which have fallen into contempt. It has failed in its first effort, because the mobs of the cities, the instrument used for its accomplishment, debased by ignorance, poverty, and vice, could not be restrained to rational action. But the world will recover from the panic of this first catastrophe."[20]

It will recover, says the Republican philosopher, because "science is progressive, and talents and enterprise on the alert." Perhaps the chief lesson to be learned is precisely that the oppressed masses of the great cities have not, by their condition, the recuperative and creative powers inherent in "the people of the country." And the next forward swing may well come from the towns and villages where the people are "more governable . . . from their principles and subordination." This above all had been the secret of the American success. This was why the Republicans had always opposed measures to advance industry as against agriculture, banking as against free trade, the city as against the country. It was no mere sentimentality for the soil, but recognition of the meaning of recurrent human experience, that led the Republicans to their conviction that liberty would flourish where industry was the handmaid of agriculture and commerce, not the center of economic life. It was legitimate to hope, Jefferson thought, that in the long future enough people in the old world, as in the new, would understand these things; that the natural aristocracy of virtue and talents would come more and more to the seats of power; "and rank, and birth, and tinsel-aristocracy . . . finally shrink into insignificance."[21]

III

Viewed as a whole, and viewed entire, the Republican philosophy is a series of variations on the theme of freedom. The policy of the moment—any moment—was devised to play a part in the development of the theme. When George Mason proposed the annual election of officers in the militia he intended to give to every man a renewed sense of his own dignity in the eyes both of God and of his fellow men. The citizen soldier was to fight for his own freedom, thereby to secure the freedom of others. He must follow orders and accept assignments, but the leaders should be of his own choosing. Organizations were to be the instruments of self-realization, not the guarantors of privilege. So also with the Constitution. The structure of government for the new republic should follow the same principle. Republicans could differ as to specific provisions, to the point of accepting or rejecting the whole, but they could not differ as to purposes. The old myth of the state was to be scrapped. Governments not only exist by the consent of the governed, they must be built to nourish consent. If they either confirmed or encouraged the privilege of some over others, if they opened the way to oppression, it was the right of the people to revolt. The American Constitution ought not to deny the right of revolution, but to obviate it. A sound domestic or foreign policy would fill in the constitutional framework with a living content of liberty. It would oppose all measures, however clever or expedient or of immediate advantage, which might, even remotely, tend to subvert freedom. Such a policy would propose only those measures which would defend freedom already won or give promise of still greater freedom. Above all, the American Republic must guarantee the unconditional divorce from the civil power of matters religious. For in religion men find their deepest and most bitter differences. If the state were to become once more, as it had so often done in the old world, a means to the advancement of one, or some, or all religions, the hope of liberty would be lost. Finally, the freedoms thus envisioned could be won and held and extended only by a people wise enough and well enough informed to know and cherish their value. At the heart of the whole system must lie education, for all, and as much for any as his abilities would warrant. Education, arising itself from free inquiry and free teaching, could be safely charged with the guardianship of its own interest.

But in the Republican scheme even freedom was to be only a condition. Beyond freedom the point was what a man did with it. The Republican wanted to improve upon it as the condition for a good life—not *the* good life. People, not *the* people, in a free republic could lead good lives, according to their many hopes and many dreams. Unity could be found in the honoring of multiplicity. Any other unity would soon or late be found to be tyrannical. The obligations and sacrifices of · citizenship were a stiff but just price for such a purpose—for anything less they were not worth assuming.

NOTES

1. Jefferson, *Writings*, IX, 334, (21 January, 1812).
2. Monroe, *Writings*, IV, 109-110, (29 November, 1803).
3. The texts of these bills, together with their legislative history, are given in *The Papers of Thomas Jefferson*, II, 526-545.
4. Jefferson, *Writings*, IV, 268, (13 August, 1786).
5. *The Papers of Thomas Jefferson*, II, 526-527, 528.
6. *Ibid.*, 531.
7. *Ibid.*, 541. As an appendix to his bill for the expansion of the College of William and Mary, Jefferson provided a chart showing the relations among the various courses to be offered.
8. Jefferson, *Writings*, IV, 268-269, (13 August, 1786).
9. Adams, *Works*, ed. C. F. Adams, 1856, X, 53, (13 July, 1813).
10. *Ibid.*, 54.
11. *Ibid.*, 53. See Zoltan Haraszti's *John Adams and the Prophets of Progress*, 1951, especially chapter V, for an illuminating account of Adams's reading of Rousseau.
12. *Ibid.*, 64.
13. *Ibid.*, 52. Napoleon did not of course, invent the word *ideology*. Earlier it had meant "the study of ideas or systems." Napoleon, in 1813, gave it the sense of "visionary theory." See Karl Mannheim, *Ideology and Utopia*, 1936, for an account of the transformations in meaning the word has undergone.
14. Dumas Malone has dealt fully and authoritatively with Jefferson's role in the French Revolution in his *Jefferson and the Rights of Man*, 1951.
15. Jefferson, *Writings*, IX, 425, (28 October, 1813).
16. *Ibid.*, italics mine.
17. *Ibid.*
18. *Ibid.*, 428.
19. *Ibid.*
20. *Ibid.*, 429.
21. *Ibid.*

Bibliographical Note

While this study is based throughout on original sources, it makes no pretense to involve the use of hitherto unpublished documents. Aside from the writings of the Republicans and other leading figures of the time, I have tried to make the best use I could of the remarkable work done by recent specialists. There is no doubt that some of the finest research and writing yet done by American historians is to be found in biographical and critical studies of such men as Jefferson and Madison. My obligation to scholars like Irving Brant and Dumas Malone must be evident throughout. My own investigations make it clear that similar work on Monroe and Gallatin, as well as lesser figures, is greatly to be desired.

The purposes of this note are to call attention to the principal works of recent scholarship which make possible studies of the sort this book represents, and to indicate the principal primary sources I have depended upon.

PRIMARY SOURCES

Debates and Proceedings in the Congress of the United States (*1789-1800*), 1834.
(Customarily cited as *Annals of Congress*).
The Works of John Adams, ed. C. F. Adams, 10 vols., 1856.
The Writings of John Quincy Adams, ed. W. C. Ford, 7 vols., 1917.
Selected Writings of John and John Quincy Adams, ed. Koch and Peden, 1946.

The Works of Fisher Ames, ed. Seth Ames, 2 vols., 1854.

The Writings of Albert Gallatin, ed. Henry Adams, 3 vols., 1879.

The Works of Alexander Hamilton, ed. H. C. Lodge, 12 vols., 1903.

Correspondence and Public Papers of John Jay, ed. H. P. Johnston, 4 vols., 1892.

The Papers of Thomas Jefferson, ed. Julian Boyd and others, 7 vols., 1949–.

The Writings of Thomas Jefferson, ed. P. L. Ford, 10 vols., 1897.

The Life and Selected Writings of Thomas Jefferson, ed. Koch and Peden, 1944.

The Works of Thomas Jefferson, ed. H. A. Washington, 9 vols., 1884.

Life and Correspondence of Rufus King, ed. C. R. King, 6 vols., 1894.

The Writings of James Madison, ed. G. Hunt, 9 vols., 1910.

The Letters and Other Writings of James Madison, Congress Edition, 4 vols., 1884.

Kate Mason Rowland, *The Life of George Mason,* 2 vols., 1892. (Contains the only published collection of Mason's speeches and writings.)

The Writings of James Monroe, ed. S. M. Hamilton, 7 vols., 1903.

Thomas Paine: Representative Selections, ed. H. H. Clark, 1944. (All the essential writings as well as the standard bibliography of Paine.)

John Taylor (of Caroline), *An Inquiry into the Principles and Policy of the Government of the United States,* 1950. (First edition, 1814.)

The Writings of George Washington, ed. J. C. Fitzpatrick, 39 vols., 1944.

The Writings of George Washington, ed. W. C. Ford, 14 vols., 1903.

The Federalist, ed. E. M. Earle, 1948.

Stuart Gerry Brown, ed. *We Hold These Truths,* 2nd edition, 1948. (Documents.)

Anson Phelps Stokes, *Church and State in the United States,* 3 vols., 1950. (A source book as well as a history.)

Memoirs of the Administrations of Washington and John Adams, from the Papers of Oliver Wolcott, ed. George Gibbs, 2 vols., 1846.

SECONDARY SOURCES

Henry Adams, *The Life of Albert Gallatin,* 1879.

Carl Becker, *The Declaration of Independence,* 1922.

Samuel F. Bemis, *Jay's Treaty*, 1924.
Albert J. Beveridge, *The Life of John Marshall*, 4 vols., 1919.
B. W. Bond, "The Monroe Mission to France, 1794-1796," *Johns Hopkins University Studies in Historical and Political Science*, XXV, 1907.
Claude Bowers, *Young Jefferson*, 1945.
Claude Bowers, *Jefferson and Hamilton*, 1925.
Claude Bowers, *Jefferson in Power*, 1936.
Irving Brant, *James Madison, the Virginia Revolutionist*, 1941.
Irving Brant, *James Madison, The Nationalist*, 1948.
Irving Brant, *James Madison, Father of the Constitution*, 1950.
Irving Brant, *James Madison, Secretary of State*, 1953.
W. P. Cresson, *James Monroe*, 1946.
Joseph S. Davis, *Essays in the Earlier History of American Corporations*, 1917.
Zoltan Haraszti, *John Adams and the Prophets of Progress*, 1951.
Helen Hill, *George Mason, Constitutionalist*, 1938.
Adrienne Koch, *Jefferson and Madison: The Great Collaboration*, 1950.
Eugene Perry Link, *Democratic-Republican Societies, 1790-1800*, 1942.
Dumas Malone, *Jefferson the Virginian*, 1948.
Dumas Malone, *Jefferson and the Rights of Man*, 1951.
Philip Marsh, *Monroe's Defense of Jefferson and Freneau against Hamilton*, 1948.
  (Reprints periodical polemics of 1792.)
John C. Miller, *Crisis in Freedom*, 1951.
Samuel Eliot Morison, *By Land and By Sea*, 1953.
  ("Elbridge Gerry, Gentleman-Democrat")
Eugene Mudge, *The Social Philosophy of John Taylor of Caroline*, 1937.
Burleigh Cushing Rodick, *American Constitutional Custom: A Forgotten Factor in the Founding*, 1953.
Nathan Schachner, *Aaron Burr*, 1937.
Nathan Schachner, *Alexander Hamilton*, 1946.
Nathan Schachner, *Thomas Jefferson*, 2 vols., 1951.
Charles Warren, *Jacobin and Junto, or Early American Politics as Viewed in the Diary of Dr. Nathaniel Ames 1758-1822*, 1931.
  (Based on the pungent records of Fisher Ames's Republican brother.)
Leonard White, *The Federalists*, 1948.
Leonard White, *The Jeffersonians*, 1951.

Appendix

Observations on Crosskey's *Politics and the Constitution*

Professor Crosskey's massive work in constitutional law and constitutional history appeared after this book was substantially written.[1] Though neither his argument nor his researches persuade me to alter my own conclusions, it is probable that I would have taken note of his work at a number of points had it been available earlier. For this reason it seems appropriate to offer some observations here.

Crosskey's intention is to make a contribution to constitutional law as currently interpreted by the Supreme Court. In this respect his work has no relation to the purposes of this book, and I have no special competence to judge of its merit. But much of his case depends upon an interpretation of the character and ideas of the early Republicans, especially Jefferson and Madison—which bears directly upon the positions set forth in these pages.

In brief, it is Crosskey's contention that Jefferson and Madison, through the instrument of the Republican Party, led a successful movement to destroy the original intent and meaning of the Constitution, on behalf of an anti-liberal, states'-rights interest. He seeks to demonstrate that the Constitution made, both by intent and by prevalent rules of construction, an almost unlimited grant of powers to the Congress, and established a Supreme Court with full jurisdiction over the common law but with no power of review (except self-protection) over the

1. William Winslow Crosskey, *Politics and the Constitution in the History of the United States,* Chicago: University of Chicago Press., 2 vols., 1953.

constitutionality of legislation. That the Constitution came to be interpreted in precisely the opposite way—as making a grant of powers to
Congress limited and enumerated only, and as establishing a Supreme
Court with no jurisdiction over the common law but with a veto over
legislation—is, according to Crosskey, owing to the chicanery of the
Republicans, even to deliberate plotting by Jefferson and Madison and
deliberate tampering with the evidence by Madison.

Crosskey's method of establishing the "true meaning" of the Constitution is to make an elaborate study of late eighteenth century usage of
legal and political terms and of principles of construction and interpretation. The materials he examines are law books—particularly Blackstone's *Commentaries*—legal and political documents both British and
American, newspapers, magazines, and other writings public and private.
By comparison of these materials he concludes, for example, that
"States" in the commerce clause ("To regulate Commerce with foreign
Nations, and among the several States, and with the Indian Tribes")
meant "the people of the states." "Commerce," he finds, meant "any
gainful activity." Thus the Constitution granted to Congress power to
legislate effectively over all matters pertaining to American economic
life. It follows from this interpretation that the judicial power could not
possibly have included a power to determine whether a particular law
is constitutional as touching an express limitation upon Congress to legislate with reference to commerce between the states. Similar interpretations of other clauses show similar grants of general power, from which
it again follows that the Supreme Court has no power of veto over
legislation. With regard to the positive powers of the Supreme Court,
Crosskey argues that "the Laws of the United States" (Art. III, Sec. 2)
meant to include the common law, by the same criteria of usage and
interpretation. Therefore the federal courts were to have full jurisdiction over common law cases—a power parallel to the power of Congress to legislate on all matters of national concern.

If such was in fact the meaning of the Constitution, the question is,
how did it come to be misunderstood and the whole course of American government perverted? Crosskey answers this question by attempting to show that both Jefferson and Madison were "apostates" from
nationalism who chose to obscure and even to obliterate the "true
meaning" when they saw dangers arising, under Federalist policies, to
the narrow sectional interests of the South with its "peculiar institution." Thus Crosskey undertakes to show that the *Federalist* was largely

a sort of hoax, written to fool anti-nationalist New Yorkers into believing that the Constitution was a prescription of limited powers—*Federalist* XLI, he says, was "bluffing." He offers, in addition, the notion that most of the *Federalist* papers were actually written only as filler to take up space in the New York papers which would otherwise have been available to opposition writers. But it is not enough to destroy the authority of the *Federalist* as a prime source of understanding the meaning of the Constitution at the time it was written. Crosskey recognizes Madison's *Notes* on the Federal Convention as the chief obstacle in his path of restoring the Constitution to its pristine meaning; so he suggests that these notes are an untruthful report. By showing what Madison "must" have known to be "true meanings," and comparing these with the notes, he finds many vital discrepancies. These can only be accounted for on the ground that Madison systematically altered his notes to conform with his later political beliefs, in effect presenting the country with rigged evidence. Crosskey takes this position without hesitation—indeed with considerable contempt for historians and lawyers who have trusted Madison in the past.

It remains to show that the Republicans actively engaged in a plot to destroy the effectiveness of the national government at its commencement. The concoction and management of this plot was, according to Crosskey, the special assignment of Jefferson—as the rigging of the evidence for future generations was the special assignment of Madison. Crosskey finds the evidence he is looking for in a series of prosecutions for libel in the federal courts of Connecticut during Jefferson's administration. The story goes this way: Behind the liberal front of allowing Federalist officeholders to remain in office as against political patronage ("We are all republicans; we are all federalists.") Jefferson took the opportunity to appoint a Republican federal district judge (Pierpont Edwards), a Republican prosecuting attorney, and to rig the federal grand jury through the appointment of Judge Edwards's son as clerk of the court. Next he ordered several libel actions to be started in the federal court under the common law. Again presenting a liberal front, Jefferson ordered these prosecutions to be tried on the basis of truth only, allowing the truth of libellous allegations to be sufficient evidence for acquittal. When these cases came before the grand jury indictments and convictions would follow. Then the prosecutor would urge appeal to the Supreme Court. This would be granted. But upon reaching the Supreme Court the cases would be thrown out, by a packed Republican court, on the ground that the common law was not a law of the United States. Thus the principle would be established that the Supreme Court was bound to declare the common law beyond the federal pale—the sole province of the states—and, by analogy, the powers of the Congress would be established as limited by the enumeration in Article I of the Constitution. The "plot," says Crosskey, succeeded—though it required about seven years for fulfilment.

In the course of his book Crosskey pays his respects to various other Rublican leaders, Gallatin, for example, appears once—in the role of a deliberate liar who made up a story about the punctuation of the welfare clause in Article I, Section 8 in order to prove that the powers of Congress are limited. Monroe is cited as favoring a conspiracy to impeach the justices of the Supreme Court during the early years of Jefferson's administration, with the clear implication that he was a narrow Southern states'-rights politician. Mason is cited, in both the Federal Convention and in the Virginia Ratifying Convention, as opposing a prohibition on *ex post facto* laws because the prohibition could be used to secure an unfair distribution of the old national debt. Thus Mason, too, is forced into the role of an enemy to national power. Crosskey's pages contain, in addition, numerous passing aspersions on the characters of Jefferson and Madison.

As a check against the very inadequate summary of Crosskey which I have given in the preceding paragraphs I recommend the reader to consult Crosskey's pages for himself. But a convenient short-cut may be found in an article by Abe Krash which begins a symposium in the Autumn 1953 number of the University of Chicago *Law Review*. Mr. Krash summarizes Crosskey in some twenty odd pages, and his treatment is sympathetic.

II

Mr. Crosskey says in his preface that he invested some thirteen years in the research and writing of the volumes now published and others yet to appear. It might well consume a year or more of another scholar's time to check Crosskey's documentation and argument and to answer his charges. Professor Charles Fairman, in an article contributed to the symposium mentioned above,[2] has undertaken to show how this would

2. Charles Fairman, "The Supreme Court and the Constitutional Limitations on State Governmental Authority," 21 *University of Chicago Law Review*, I, 40-78.

have to be done. Fairman examines one only of Crosskey's many contentions, that Amendments II through IX were intended to apply to the states as well as the federal government. His method is to examine the positions taken by members of the First Congress, which passed the Amendments, in various state constitutional conventions held after the Amendments were adopted. The record shows that these men, without exception, contributed to the drafting of state bills of rights which would have been without meaning had the federal Amendments been understood as binding against the states.

I make no pretense to have made an exhaustive analysis and check upon Crosskey's book. But certain major observations are admissible on the basis of well-known evidence. The fact is that Crosskey has written a very long and often brilliant brief for the prosecution in the imaginary case of *United States v. Jefferson, Madison, et al.* In literary terms it is fair to say that he conducts a long debate with the dead. But however one chooses to characterize the performance, the central fact is that he has selected such evidence as seems to him to confirm his argument, and ignored or given only partial treatment to other evidence which would disprove his positions. I can offer here a few examples only, but they are obviously crucial. I should perhaps add that I am not a lawyer, nor do the defendants require the services of me or anyone else in their defense.

1) It is essential for Crosskey's argument to show that Madison understood in 1787-1788 that the Constitution was an instrument for broad national power without enumerated limitation upon Congress. The materials he uses are, for the most part, the well-known facts which have recently been definitively collected, augmented, and set forth in the second and third volumes of Irving Brant's standard life of Madison —*James Madison, The Nationalist* (1948) and *James Madison, Father of the Constitution* (1950). It is, by the way, characteristic of Crosskey's book that it entirely ignores scholarship of this kind. What these facts show is that Madison recognized fully the weaknesses of a loose federation such as the Articles of Confederation established, and wished to strengthen the national government by the achievement of a delicate balance between national and state power. His primary concern was assuredly for the United States, but his profound belief was that freedom was dependent upon a wise distribution of power, both by the separation of powers in the national government and by the assignment of certain powers only to the national government and the reservation

of others to the states. By emphasizing Madison's willingness to grant
very great power—especially the power of direct taxation—to the federal government, and ignoring his views on reservation, Crosskey manages to convey a picture of Madison which is heavily documented but
leaves him only a part of the man he was. Thus a simple reference to
Madison's correspondence with Jefferson regarding a bill of rights will
remove the distortion Crosskey has effected. This matter is considered
in Chapter II of the present book. The reader will remember that Madison attempted to reassure Jefferson by arguing that a bill of rights was
unnecessary in a government of limited and enumerated powers. His
position was simply that the federal government could not think of
infringing on the rights of citizens because it had no powers other than
those enumerated, and such powers of infringing were not included in
the enumeration. It will be remembered that James Wilson took the
same position—indeed Madison was defending Wilson's view as well as
his own. This ground is, of course, precisely the ground that the Republicans took in such matters as the debate over a national bank and
their attack on the Sedition Act. Read in its proper context, with full
reference to both the nationalist and "states'-rights" aspects of Madison's
thinking, *Federalist* XLI is anything but a "bluff." The point is that,
from the beginning, Madison was dealing with delicate problems of
political compromise, with the hope, never surrendered, of achieving
both strength and liberty in America. *Federalist* X remains the classic
statement of the position.

2) In his handling of Madison's *Notes* on the Federal Convention
Crosskey reads these back into the political history of the United States
after the Constitution was adopted. By the process of careful selection
he emphasizes all aspects of Madison's politics which bear upon the
protection of liberty as against the national government, in such a way
that Madison appears to have been an "apostate" to the pure nationalism
of his early life which Crosskey has "demonstrated" by the same technique. Thus the *Notes* appear to have been doctored to fit a later political position, because they do not support the original contention that
Madison, along with the other framers, understood the Constitution as
an unlimited grant. Again, a simple reference to Madison's writing, in
precisely those later years when we are to imagine him tampering with
his own records of the Constitutional Convention, will remove the distortion. Crosskey makes no reference to Madison's repeated and earnest
efforts to disassociate himself from the "Nullifiers" and to cut the

ground from under them by appeal to his own authority as a framer. In his *Notes on Nullification* (1835-1836), as well as countless other documents with which all students are familiar, Madison argues over and over again, and with consummate skill, against precisely the states'-rights interpretation which Crosskey accuses him of supporting. I have dealt with this matter in Chapter II above.

3) Crosskey argues that the Virginia and Kentucky Resolutions of 1798 reveal Jefferson and Madison in their true colors as perpetrators of fraud. He considers these documents as directly subversive and the Sedition Act against which they were directed as a legitimate use of the powers of Congress. In particular, he argues that the case built by Jefferson, Madison and other Republicans against the act because it allowed "truth" to stand as sufficient evidence for acquittal, was a sham—and owing to their fear of being held to the truth in the courts. Again Crosskey's method is to select his evidence in the manner of a lawyer's brief. What he ignores is in fact the heart of the matter. As I have shown in Chapter II, what worried the Republicans was not their inability to prove the truth of factual allegations but the "truth" of *opinions*. Since the truth was to be the test of guilt, it followed that a man who could not prove the truth of his *opinions* would be punished. And how was the "truth" to be determined? The method under the law was to convince a jury and court which might well disagree with the opinions under indictment. Further, if the national government (or any other) could determine the truth of alleged libellous opinions, it could determine the truth of opinions of any kind including religious. When the Republican position on the Sedition Law is studied *as a whole*,[3] it is clear that it was a magnificent defense of precisely those individual freedoms for which the Revolution was fought and which have always to be defended against the encroachments of government or self-appointed judges of orthodoxy. Further, Crosskey deals not at all with Madison's repeated denunciation of the States'-Righters of the 1830's for their attempt to use his name and the name of Jefferson in their distortion of the Kentucky and Virginia Resolutions. It is no exaggeration to say that Madison was more fearful of Calhoun and what he represented in America than he was of the abolitionists.

---

3. See, for example, A. Koch and H. Ammon, "The Virginia and Kentucky Resolutions: An Episode in Jefferson's and Madison's Defense of Civil Liberties," *William and Mary Quarterly*, April, 1948 147-176.

4) Crosskey's contention that Amendments II-IX were understood by the members of the First Congress as binding against the states has already been amply refuted by Fairman in the article cited above. But it is worth pointing out that the clause in Madison's first draft of the First Amendment, which would have made the prohibition on legislation with reference to the freedoms of speech and religion binding against the states, in explicit language, was defeated in the Congress. Madison, in the passage from the Congressional debates quoted in Chapter V, made it abundantly clear that he thought the defeated provision was the central point in the whole effort. His forthright statement is simply not to be reconciled by any sophistry with the notion that he understood the amendments as applying equally to the states.

5) As a final note on Crosskey's systematic abuse of Madison it is enough to observe that wherever the notes on the Constitutional Convention seem to support Crosskey's argument they are treated as genuine; where they do not fit the argument, or directly contradict it, they are implied or asserted to be spurious.

6) I am content to pass over the long argument by which Crosskey would persuade us that the decision of the Supreme Court to leave the common law to the states was the result of a plot by Jefferson and his Republican cohorts. The story is inherently incredible. For one thing it supposes that Jefferson was prepared to risk bringing his crucial point to test before a Supreme Court which was solidly Federalist, as it was at the time of the Connecticut prosecutions, or else that he ordered the actions to be commenced at a time when it might be necessary to wait many years before he could pack the Court with Republicans as Federalist judges died. For another thing, it asks us to believe that Jefferson understood the national government to have the broadest powers at the very time he was asking for constitutional amendments to provide such power for the executive to purchase Louisiana and for the Congress to enact the program of internal improvements, on the ground that the powers of government were all limited and enumerated. As for the "truth" of the Backus libel (one of the Connecticut cases), of which Crosskey makes great substance in order to destroy Jefferson's personal character, it is enough to say that Jefferson admitted his improper advances to Mrs. Walker, which had occurred almost forty years before, and yet managed to survive the Federalist attempts at character assassination. There does not, in any case, appear to be a very close connection between Jefferson's youthful indiscretion and a "correct" interpretation of the Constitution.

7) A brief comment may be made on the role of Monroe as a Republican "conspirator" against the Constitution. It is certainly true, as Crosskey states, that Monroe favored the impeachment of Justice Chase. The record of that judge's court in the sedition trials would seem to provide ample warrant for the Republican view.[4] But there was nothing secret or conspiratorial about Monroe's attitude in the matter—or that of any other Republican. Chase was acquitted only because the Republicans were unable to carry the Senate in 1800, and the Federalists used that body, as they used the Supreme Court, to frustrate the expressed will of the people. It is also beyond question that Monroe conceived the federal government as a limited instrument and approved it as such, both in the early days and during his presidency. What Crosskey omits in his study is the evidence that Monroe wished a stronger, not a weaker, federal government. Crosskey does not mention Monroe's long pamphlet on the draft Constitution, written in 1788, which is discussed in detail in Chapter II above. This document criticised the Constitution principally on the ground that it might *not* overcome the weaknesses of the Confederation, that the powers of the states remained too great for the safety of the nation.

8) A similar observation is appropriate in the case of Mason. Crosskey cites Mason only in connection with the prohibition against *ex post facto laws*. Mason opposed this provision, and suggested that it might well make a fair distribution of the public debt impossible. But this view can only be interpreted in the narrow interest of states'-rights when considered out of context. Obviously to allow the Congress to enact *ex post facto* legislation, which Mason favored, would greatly increase the national power. Mason was certainly intelligent enough to see that such power could be used *against* the special interests of the Southern states as well as for them, yet he was quite willing to risk such an eventuality. As in the case of Monroe, Crosskey also omits to mention an important document expressing a view which does not support his thesis. Mason's paper, "Objections to this Constitution of Government," also discussed in Chapter II above, like Monroe's, criticises the draft Constitution on the ground that it provides a national power inadequate as against the states.

4. See on this and other aspects of Federalist behavior John C. Miller, *Crisis in Freedom*, 1951.

9) Crosskey's inferential inclusion of Gallatin in a conspiracy to protect slavery is not worthy of notice. But one may wonder why John Quincy Adams, a Republican by conversion, was not similarly honored.

10) Crosskey indicates in his title and in many places throughout his book that he considers *politics* as the cause of that perversion of the Constitution he seeks to demonstrate. Yet, over and above the kind of historical distortion I have been noticing here, it is precisely the function of politics which the book ignores or fails to understand. In the proper sense of the term Crosskey does not actually deal with politics at all. His approach to his materials is that of a lawyer, an exceedingly competent lawyer. But no amount of legal hair-splitting and logic-chopping has ever succeeded as a substitute for the political process in America.

This defect occurs at several levels in Crosskey's book. For example, he constantly refers to men like Wilson, Hamilton, and Gouverneur Morris (whom, by the way, he makes the chief author of the Constitution) as men trained in the law who *must* have been thinking in terms of Blackstone. Thus the Constitution, following Blackstone's principles of legal construction and interpretation, *must have meant*, etc. Yet Crosskey seems unaware of the fact that such leading delegates as Franklin, Mason, Gerry, and Madison himself were not lawyers but politicians.

The difficulty is more serious at the level of characterizing the debates of the convention. These were not arguments in a judicial proceeding; they were the energetic giving and taking, pulling and hauling, of political struggle and controversy. When delegates referred to the "states" they were not applying any rules of construction whatever; they were simply talking of the regions from which they came, the political and geographical entities whose credentials they held, whose interests they were bound to represent, and which had formed the Confederation that was under revision. The motives which guided the delegates were political motives—jealousy of individual liberty or group privilege, solicitude for state powers and prerogatives, ideal conceptions of a nation, greater or lesser trust in the people, concern for the common security against invasion, desire to manipulate power, and recognition of the need for compromise. Given the actual situation of the American states —with reference to one another, to their Confederation, to the outside world, to their economic plight, and to their cultural, religious, economic, and political differences—anything other than the complex and limited constitutional government on which the delegates eventually agreed would have been utterly impossible. The formulation of the Constitution was a heroic *political* achievement, the most remarkable product of a free political process in modern history. It was heroic because it managed the nearly impossible by appealing just enough to both national and sectional interests and prejudices to be adopted. The technique was the technique which makes democracy the supreme mode of human expression—the politics of compromise, in which the honor and loyalty of all are maintained by permitting the domination of none. It was in guiding this process that Madison made his invaluable contribution—not as a nationalist merely, or a sectionalist merely, but as a democratic politician. This is why he is properly called the "Father of the Constitution."

As the Constitution was the product of political controversy and compromise among individuals and factions, so too the interpretation of the Constitution, after it became effective, was and is a matter of politics. Of course politicians would appeal to Blackstone's principles, if these showed promise of political effectiveness; of course strict construction would be applied in extreme terms, if politicians (including Madison) thought it might achieve a partisan purpose. The Constitution, because it is a political document kept alive by generations of people living in a political process, cannot have a fixed and certain meaning. Otherwise it would be dead, and the nation with it. What matters is that, whether our construction be loose or strict, we keep alive the republican spirit of Jefferson and Madison and, using the Constitution as the foundation of individual liberty, keep alive with it the promise of American life.